THE LITTLE GUIDES
REPTILES
& AMPHIBIANS

THE LITTLE GUIDES

REPTILES

& AMPHIBIANS

CONSULTANT EDITOR

Dr. Harold G. Cogger

FOG CITY PRESS

Published by Fog City Press
814 Montgomery Street
San Francisco, CA 94133 USA
Reprinted in 2000 (three times), 2001

Chief Executive Officer: John Owen
President: Terry Newell
Publisher: Lynn Humphries
Managing Editor: Janine Flew
Art Director: Kylie Mulquin
Editorial Coordinator: Tracey Gibson
Production Manager: Martha Malic-Chavez
Business Manager: Emily Jahn
Vice President International Sales: Stuart Laurence

Project Editor: Jane Bowring
Designer: Eilish Bouchier
Consultant Editor: Dr. Harold G. Cogger

A catalog record for this book is available from
the Library of Congress, Washington, DC.

ISBN 1 875137 58 0

Color reproduction by Colourscan Co Pte Ltd
Printed by LeeFung-Asco Printers
Printed in China

A Weldon Owen Production

CONTENTS

PART THREE
KINDS OF REPTILES

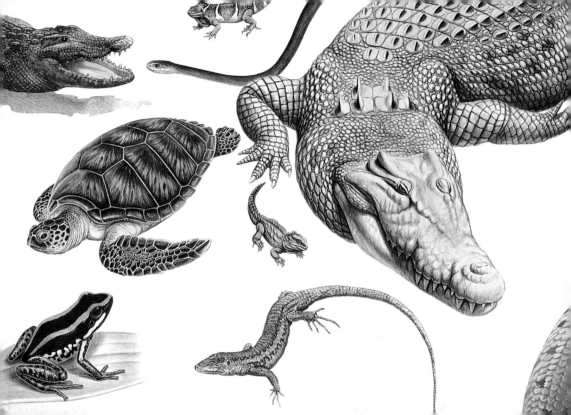

PART ONE

THE WORLD OF REPTILES AND AMPHIBIANS

INTRODUCING REPTILES
AND
AMPHIBIANS

The ancestors of today's amphibians were the first vertebrate animals to leave the water and spend some of their time on land. Their eggs, however, like those of their modern descendants, lacked a protective shell so they still needed water or very moist environments to complete their life cycle. The first reptiles evolved from these amphibians, taking the conquest of the land one stage further. With their dry, scaly skin and leathery-shelled eggs, the reptiles could survive on land without returning to the water. Today's reptiles and amphibians inhabit astonishingly varied environments, exhibiting diverse forms and a fascinating array of complex behavior.

WHAT ARE REPTILES AND AMPHIBIANS?

Reptiles and amphibians, along with birds, fish and mammals, belong to a group of animals known as vertebrates. Vertebrates have a bony backbone, which is a strong, flexible column to which other body structures are attached.

Classifying animals Scientists arrange animals in groups which are based on common characteristics and evolutionary descent. Animal classes, such as reptiles and amphibians, are divided into orders, families, genera and species (going from the most general to the most specific). There are three orders of living amphibians and four of reptiles. The differences between reptiles and amphibians are generally more obvious than their similarities, but their joint study under the name "herpetology" is a scientific tradition dating back nearly two centuries.

Amphibian orders The three amphibian orders are salamanders and newts (order Caudata); caecilians (order Gymnophiona); and frogs and toads (order Anura).

Reptile orders The four reptile orders are turtles and tortoises (order Testudinata); crocodiles and alligators (order Crocodilia); tuataras (order Rhynchocephalia); and snakes, lizards and amphisbaenians (order Squamata). The squamates are divided into three suborders: Sauria (lizards), Serpentes (snakes) and Amphisbaenia (amphisbaenians).

Species diversity There are 7,400 species of living reptiles. The reptiles have evolved adaptations to suit almost every habitat in the temperate and tropical regions of the world. They therefore vary enormously in size and structure. Because of their greater dependence on moisture, the amphibians tend to be less diverse in shape and size. There are 4,950 species of living amphibians. In both groups, there are many species that are unremarkable in color, but others rival the birds with their bold, bright patterns and gaudy hues.

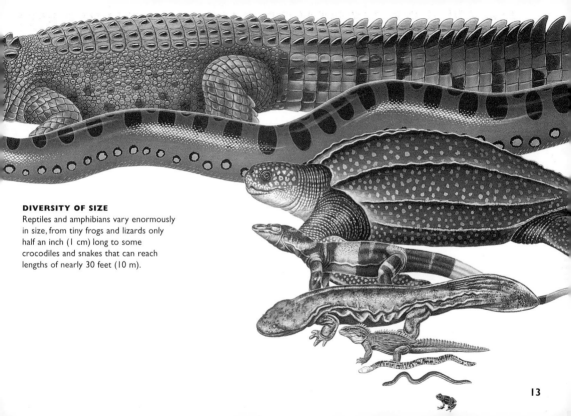

DIVERSITY OF SIZE

Reptiles and amphibians vary enormously in size, from tiny frogs and lizards only half an inch (1 cm) long to some crocodiles and snakes that can reach lengths of nearly 30 feet (10 m).

13

TEMPERATURE CONTROL

When a lizard moves out from under a crevice and lies on a rock in the early morning sun, it is warming itself so it can become active enough to escape predators while searching for food. Reptiles and amphibians are unable to control their body temperature by internal, physiological means and must rely on external sources of heat. This is why they are often called "cold-blooded."

SHADES OF THE DAY

Many reptiles and amphibians can regulate their body temperature by changing the color of their skin. In the early morning and late afternoon, the skin of these rhinoceros iguanas is dark so it absorbs the heat of the sun. During the hottest parts of the day, their skin becomes lighter, helping them to reflect as much heat as possible.

Every activity of an animal's life—hatching, feeding, reproducing, escaping from predators, even just moving about—depends on it having a body temperature that allows it to function normally. This temperature varies from species to species, but the temperatures at which most reptiles and amphibians function best range from 68° to 86°F (20°C to 30°C). This means that they are most abundant in the warm temperate and tropical regions of the world.

Reptile behavior Reptiles and amphibians regulate their temperature by their behavior. Many lizards, for example, warm up by moving into the sun or onto a warm surface and exposing as much of their body as they can to the heat. To cool down, they expose as little of their body as possible to the heat, or they move into the shade or to a

An American alligator suns itself on a log.

cooler place, such as a crevice or a burrow. Not all reptiles, however, behave like this. There are tropical lizards and snakes which are active at night because the night-time temperatures are mild and constant.

Amphibian behavior Most amphibians are nocturnal and are only active when their surroundings are moist enough to stop them becoming dehydrated. However some frogs in cooler climates do bask to raise their body temperature, but only if they live near water as

basking results in moisture loss. Tiger salamanders and tadpoles in many parts of the world increase their temperature by moving into shallow water on sunny days.

Shutting down While being "cold-blooded" can have disadvantages, such as being sluggish at low temperatures and therefore more vulnerable to predators, it also has advantages. Amphibians and reptiles can "shut down" when conditions are unsuitable. In colder climates,

lizards and frogs hibernate underground during the winter. Alligators can survive freezing temperatures in shallow pools as long as they keep their noses above the water so that breathing holes form when the water freezes. Temperatures which are too high can be just as lethal as the cold. In hot desert regions, frogs are active during the cooler parts of the year but burrow underground to avoid the heat of the summer and because no moisture is available. This is called "estivation."

A pink agama lizard from Africa basks on a rock. Reptiles change their behavior to adjust to temperature.

SKIN AND SCALES

Soft and smooth, hard and dry—the skin of amphibians and the skin of reptiles differ markedly, but in both cases it is a fascinating organ with many unusual functions.

Amphibian skin The skin of most amphibians is thin and needs to be kept moist to function effectively. One of its important functions is water balance: the skin is highly permeable, allowing water to be absorbed or lost. Most amphibians have lungs, but respiration, the process by which animals take up oxygen and give off carbon dioxide, also occurs through the skin. There are many glands in an amphibian's skin. Secretions from the mucous glands keep the skin moist. Other glands secrete the poisons with which many species defend themselves.

Reptile skin The outer layer of a reptile's skin is thickened to form scales. Crests, knobs, warts and other bumps are areas where the skin has thickened even more. A reptile's scales are dry, coarse and watertight so their bodies won't dry out. The ability of some reptiles to change color can play an important part in defense, mating and temperature regulation. Skin color and color changes are caused by pigment cells just below the outer layers of the skin.

Shedding skin All reptiles and many amphibians shed their skin from time to time. Some frogs shed their skin every few days, some snakes only once a year. Sometimes the skin comes away in small bits and pieces, sometimes in larger fragments. Crocodilians just lose isolated horny scutes, whereas many snakes and lizards and some salamanders shed the whole skin in one go.

This Pacific giant salamander has smooth, shiny skin which, as with all salamanders and newts, must be kept moist at all times.

SNAKE PEEL

To loosen its skin, a snake rubs its nose against a hard surface and then it wriggles free. The old skin, including the snake's eyelids, comes off inside out. This old keratin layer is not shed until a new one has completely formed underneath it.

REPRODUCTION AND LIFECYCLES

The eggs of amphibians are typically gelatinous capsules inside which the embryo develops before breaking out to become a free-living tadpole. A reptile egg is typically covered with a hard or leathery shell inside which the young develops until it hatches as a fully formed and independent replica of its parents.

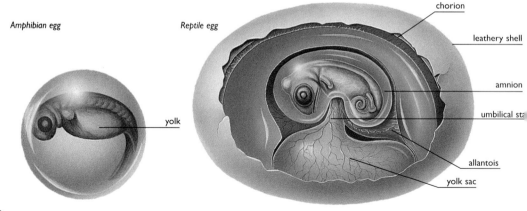

Amphibian egg

Reptile egg

yolk

chorion

leathery shell

amnion

umbilical sta

allantois

yolk sac

Different lifecycles Reptiles produce eggs within which the embryo develops and then hatches (or is born, in the case of live-bearing species) into what is generally a miniature replica of the adult. Amphibians, however, have a two-stage lifecycle. The eggs hatch into aquatic larvae, such as tadpoles, which often differ markedly from the adult. The larvae have gills, take in oxygen from the water, and eventually metamorphose into adults which breathe air and live mostly on land. Occasionally the entire tadpole stage takes place within the egg or within the mother's body.

Amphibian eggs Amphibians lay eggs varying in number from a single egg to many thousands laid in clutches. The eggs do not have a waterproof covering and are always laid in water or damp places so they do not dry out. Each fertilized egg is surrounded by a dense protective jelly, and contains yolk to nourish the developing young. The waste products simply permeate out through the jelly.

Reptilian eggs The reptile egg is more complex than the amphibian egg. It has a hard waterproof shell which enables the young to develop on dry land. Oxygen enters the egg through a sac called the chorion, just beneath the eggshell. The yolk sac nourishes the embryo and its waste is stored in a another sac called the allantois. The embryo is cushioned by the amnion, a fluid-filled sac which also prevents the embryo from drying out. This kind of egg is a closed system in which all the embryo's needs are met, allowing it to grow into a miniature adult. In those reptiles where the young develop inside the mother's body, the eggs do not have a shell but the various sacs function in the same way.

Fertilization Amphibians fertilize their eggs both internally and externally. Most frogs fertilize externally. The male clasps the female with his forelimbs and, as she lays the eggs, expels his sperm over them. Most salamanders fertilize their eggs internally. The male deposits a package of sperm which is picked up by the female's cloacal lips and stored in her cloaca until needed for fertilization. This may occur immediately or be delayed for months or even years. Reptile eggs are always fertilized internally. With the exception of the tuatara, where fertilization occurs through cloacal contact, all male reptiles have well-developed organs for inseminating the females.

Single parents Some chameleons, dragon lizards, night lizards, whiptail lizards wall lizards and geckos reproduce without males. The eggs of these lizards do not need to be fertilized. These all-female lizards increase in number faster than those that have male and female parents.

AMPHIBIAN HABITATS

The word amphibian comes from the Greek word "amphibios" which means "a being with a double life." Most amphibians do indeed live two different lives—in water as larvae and on land as adults—but some live their whole lives in water and others never leave the land.

The North American bullfrog is common and widespread, favoring marshes and wetlands of any kind.

Salamanders are widespread, although most are found in the Northern Hemisphere. The fire salamander Salamandra salamandra (left) occurs in Europe and north-west Africa.

Salamanders and newts Most salamanders and newts live in cool, shady places in regions with temperate climates. They live in a variety of habitats, but all are damp or wet. Aquatic species can be found in rivers, lakes, mountain streams, swamps and underground caves.

Some, like sirens, congo eels and the olm, are almost limbless and swim like snakes. Others, like the giant salamanders, hellbenders and mudpuppies, have normal limbs and crawl about on the bottoms of lakes and rivers. Terrestrial species usually live under rocks and logs, but some burrow into the soil and others live in trees.

Caecilians These legless, worm-like creatures usually live underground in tropical forests and plantations. They move along tunnels they build by

A Great Plains toad burrows into the sand.

pushing their head through loose mud or damp soil. All caecilians burrow, even the aquatic ones which burrow into the soft mud and gravel on the floor of their watery habitats.

Frogs and toads The most numerous and diverse of the amphibians, frogs and toads can be found in nearly all habitats, from deserts, savannas and mountains to tropical rainforests. Most live in water for at least part of their lives, usually the tadpole stage. Nearly all frogs can swim though some are better at it than others. On land frogs can be found under logs, amongst the leaf litter on forest floors, or in damp rock crevices. Some burrow into soft dirt or mud either for daytime retreats or for long periods of aestivation during very dry seasons. Australian water-holding frogs, for example, spend most of their life buried deep in the ground, emerging only when it rains to breed. Other frogs live in shrubs and

ADAPTED FOR CLIMBING
Treefrogs are much flatter than frogs that live on the ground. This distributes the weight evenly over their whole body, enabling them to balance and move with great agility on branches and leaves. Special finger and toe pads help them adhere to smooth surfaces and they move about by grasping branches or leaping from one perch to another.

trees. Some tree-dwellers lay their eggs in tree holes or in the base of epiphytic plants so the tadpoles can live in the pools that collect there.

REPTILE HABITATS

There are reptiles in nearly every habitat on Earth. They live in rainforests, woodlands, savannas, grasslands, mountains, deserts and scrub. They can be found on the ground, under the ground, in trees and in water, and some even take to the air from time to time.

Turtles and tortoises Sea turtles live in temperate and tropical oceans. Freshwater turtles occur in still water, such as ponds and lakes, and in running streams and rivers. The sea turtles and a few species of freshwater turtles leave their aquatic habitats only to lay eggs. The other species are amphibious and regularly move about on land. There are a few land tortoises that live in dry areas where there are no open bodies of water.

Tuatara The tuatara lives in areas of low forest and scrub, spending its day in burrows on the forest floor.

Crocodilians All crocodilians are semi-aquatic and do not venture far from water. Most species favor the warm, still water of lakes, ponds, swamps or the lower reaches of rivers, while a few prefer the cool, clear water of running rivers. Most crocodilians live in freshwater habitats, but a few are at home in the more saline environments of mangrove swamps and estuaries.

Lizards Lizards are found in almost all habitats. Some live in temperate climates, some in extremely hot or cold areas, and some experience both extremes in different seasons. Most lizards are terrestrial or tree-dwelling. They shelter in all sorts of places—in cracks and crevices, under rocks and logs, amongst leaf litter or clumps of vegetation, in holes in tree trunks or in the foliage—and some burrow into the ground. A few lizards are semi-aquatic, retreating to water when disturbed. The marine iguana is the only lizard which enters the sea.

Lizards are especially numerous in arid regions. This desert iguana lives in the dry areas of southern USA and Mexico.

Amphisbaenians Worm lizards spend most of their lives underground. They prefer moist habitats in which to build their tunnels, but some burrow through very hard soils.

Snakes Snakes occur on almost all parts of the planet except the very coldest areas and they live in all kinds of habitats. Most live on the ground, but many live in trees, beneath the ground in burrows or in fresh or sea water. Some, like the anaconda which lies in wait at the water's edge for prey, are semi-aquatic. Others, such as the file snakes, are totally aquatic.

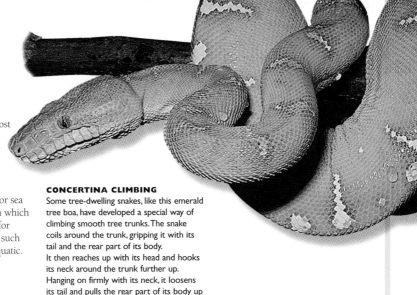

CONCERTINA CLIMBING

Some tree-dwelling snakes, like this emerald tree boa, have developed a special way of climbing smooth tree trunks. The snake coils around the trunk, gripping it with its tail and the rear part of its body.
It then reaches up with its head and hooks its neck around the trunk further up. Hanging on firmly with its neck, it loosens its tail and pulls the rear part of its body up to near the neck. Repeating this process, it can climb up the smooth trunk of the tree.

The eastern box turtle lives in moist forests and grasslands.

DISTRIBUTION

Amphibians occur throughout much of the world. The only places where native amphibians do not occur are Antarctica, the northernmost parts of Europe, Asia and North America, and most oceanic islands. Reptiles live on all continents except Antarctica and some can be found on tiny remote islands. Being ectothermic, the number of species decreases toward higher latitudes and elevations. Nevertheless, the hardy viviparous lizard and the European viper occur above the Arctic Circle in Scandinavia, and on some mountains lizards skirt around snow banks in their daily activities.

SALAMANDERS AND NEWTS
Almost all salamanders and newts (caudates) are found in the Northern Hemisphere—in Europe, central and northern Asia, north-western Africa, North America and Mexico. A few species occur in South-East Asia and in South America as far south as central Bolivia and southern Brazil. Caudates are found from sea level to about 14,700 feet (4,500 m). Most occur in temperate regions though the lungless salamanders occur in tropical parts of Central and South America.

The two-lined salamander is found near brooks and springs in central to eastern North America.

CAECILIANS

Caecilians are confined to tropical and subtropical regions of the world. In Asia they can be found in southern China, southern Philippines, South-East Asia, Sri Lanka and India. Elsewhere they occur in equatorial East and West Africa, the Seychelles and in tropical Central and South America.

FROGS AND TOADS

There are frogs and toads on most islands and on every continent except Antarctica. Three species—the common frog and moor frog of Europe, and the wood frog of North America—have ranges which extend north of the Arctic Circle. While many frogs and toads have successfully colonized the temperate regions, more than 80 percent of species are found in the tropics and subtropics.

TURTLES AND TORTOISES

Turtles and tortoises live in the temperate and tropical regions of the world. Hidden-necked turtles are found on all continents except Antarctica and in all the oceans. Side-necked turtles are found only in Australasia, South America, and central and southern Africa.

DISTRIBUTION continued

TUATARAS

Tuataras once ranged throughout the two main islands of New Zealand but are now restricted to 30 small islands off the north-east coast of the North Island and in Cook Strait.

CROCODILIANS

Most crocodilian species occur in tropical parts of the world, but a few, notably the American and Chinese alligators, extend into temperate regions. Alligators and caimans are found in south-eastern USA, Central and South America and eastern China. Crocodiles are found in Africa, Madagascar, Asia, Australia and Central and South America. The false gharial occurs in South-East Asia and the gharial in India, Pakistan, Nepal and Bangladesh.

The Malagasy chameleon of Madagascar is usually dull green when resting among foliage, but takes on this striking pattern when disturbed.

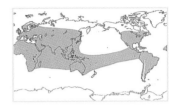

LIZARDS

Lizards today occupy almost all landmasses except Antarctica and some Arctic regions of North America, Europe and Asia. Species occur from sea level up to 16,500 feet (5,000 m). They are particularly numerous in hot, arid parts of the world, but many also occur in temperate climates.

AMPHISBAENIANS

Most species live in Central and South America and Africa, but there are a few species in the West Indies and the warmer parts of North America (Florida), the Middle East and Europe (Spain).

SNAKES

Snakes inhabit most parts of the planet outside the polar regions, from alpine meadows to the tropical Pacific and Indian oceans. They occupy all landmasses with the exception of Iceland, Ireland, New Zealand and some small oceanic islands.

THE ORIGINS OF REPTILES AND AMPHIBIANS

The first backboned animals evolved in the sea about 500 million years ago. During the next 150 million years they continued to evolve into amazingly diverse groups of fishes. But to colonize the land these animals had to overcome the tremendous challenges involved in exchanging a totally aquatic life for a terrestrial one. These challenges included obtaining oxygen from the air rather than water, abandoning the buoyancy of water and modifying the body to cope with the high gravitational forces encountered on land.

FIRST AMPHIBIANS AND EARLY REPTILE.

The first vertebrates to make the transition from water to land were the amphibians. About 360 million years ago they became the first tetrapods; that is, the first backboned animals with four jointed limbs. It was from these animals that reptiles, birds and mammals evolved.

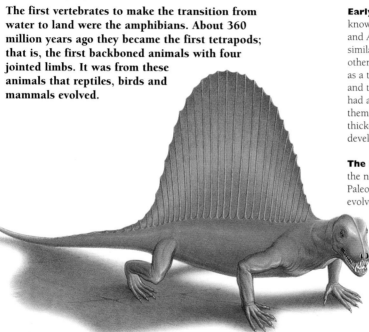

Early amphibians The earliest known amphibians were *Ichthyostega* and *Acanthostega*. They had a skull similar to their fish ancestors and other fish-like characteristics such as a tail fin and scales in the belly and tail. However, unlike fish, they had a short neck and, to support them on land, four limbs, a greatly thickened backbone and a well-developed rib cage.

The age of amphibians Over the next 100 million years, the late Paleozoic period, the amphibians evolved into many diverse forms and became the dominant animals of the day. Some were enormous, reaching 13 feet (4 m) in length, others were quite bizarre. Many were aquatic and possessed gills, but many more made the transition to land.

FIRST ON LAND

Acanthostega (right) and *Icthyostega* (below far right) had strong limbs, indicating their shallow-water or even terrestrial habits. However the fish-like characteristics they retained suggest that they probably never ventured far from water. They would have moved awkwardly on land whereas their heavy bodies would have been buoyant in water and their finned tail would have propelled them along with ease.

SOME EARLY REPTILES

The first reptiles, like *Hylonomus* (below), were small lizard-like animals that hunted insects and small amphibians. Some later reptiles, like *Dimetrodon* (far left), looked like dinosaurs but were related to the ancestors of mammals. *Coelurosauravus* (left) had flaps of skin attached to its ribs which enabled it to glide from tree to tree much like the flying lizard of today.

The first reptiles

About 50 million years after the first amphibians appeared, the first reptiles evolved from an amphibian ancestor. The development of an egg with a waterproof shell meant that the reptiles had a much better chance of surviving on land. Another 100 million years on they had replaced the amphibians as the dominant land-dwelling animals. This was the beginning of the age of the dinosaurs, by which time most of the ancient amphibians were extinct.

Modern amphibians There are no fossil records linking the amphibians of today to the ancient Paleozoic forms so their direct ancestors are unknown. The first frog fossil, from Madagascar, is 245 million years old; the first salamander fossil, found in Russia, 150 million years old; and the first caecilian fossil 65 million years old.

31

THE AGE OF THE DINOSAURS

The early reptiles evolved into turtles and tortoises, lizards, crocodiles, birds and dinosaurs. For 140 million years, the dinosaurs dominated the Earth. Their reign came to an abrupt end when, around 65 million years ago, a catastrophic event wiped them out along with most of the other large reptiles except the crocodiles and turtles.

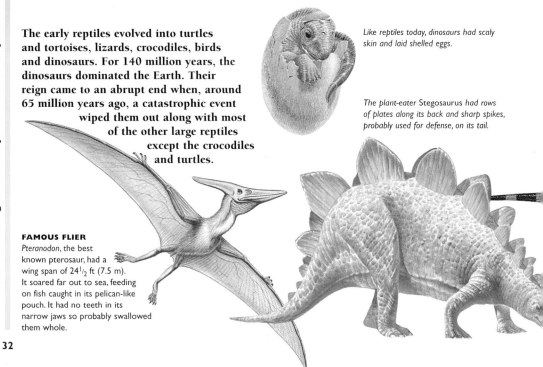

Like reptiles today, dinosaurs had scaly skin and laid shelled eggs.

The plant-eater Stegosaurus had rows of plates along its back and sharp spikes, probably used for defense, on its tail.

FAMOUS FLIER
Pteranodon, the best known pterosaur, had a wing span of 24$^1/_2$ ft (7.5 m). It soared far out to sea, feeding on fish caught in its pelican-like pouch. It had no teeth in its narrow jaws so probably swallowed them whole.

Amazing animals Dinosaurs are well known for their often bizarre appearance. Some were the size of chickens; others may have been as long as a jumbo jet. They are divided into two groups, depending on how their hip bones were arranged: the Saurischia had a reptile-like pelvis and the Ornithischia had a bird-like pelvis. Some dinosaurs walked on two legs, though most used four. The Ornithischia were all plant-eaters. Some of the Saurischia evolved into the biggest meat-eaters the world has ever known, fierce hunters like *Allosaurus* and *Tyrannosaurus*. Others became plant-eating giants. *Diplodocus* reached a length of 100 feet (30 m) and *Brachiosaurus* was 65 feet (20 m) long and stood 40 feet (12 m) high.

Distant cousins While dinosaurs ruled the land, marine reptiles such as plesiosaurs, pliosaurs, turtles and crocodiles dominated the sea. The sky was the domain of pterosaurs, the first backboned animals to take to the air. They had wings of skin which were supported by their greatly elongated fourth fingers and attached to their body at thigh level.

An active, agile predator, Deinonychus grabbed its prey with its long forelimbs and disembowelled it with the sharp claws on its hindlimbs.

Proganochelys, *from the dinosaur age, had much in common with living tortoises.*

LATER REPTILES

While the dinosaurs died out, along with other ruling reptiles such as the pterosaurs, ichthyosaurs and plesiosaurs, the ancestors of today's reptiles survived and evolved into thousands of different species. The only living representatives of those original ruling reptiles, the archosaurs, are the crocodiles.

FIVE AQUATIC CRETACEANS

From left to right: Platycarpus was a marine lizard with a tail as long as its body. *Elasmosaurus*, a 46-ft (14-m) plesiosaur, had the longest neck of any marine reptile. *Archelon*, a huge turtle almost 13 ft (4 m) long, had weak jaws and a toothless beak so probably ate jellyfish like the leatherback turtle today. *Deinosuchus*, a 49-ft (15-m) giant could have been the largest crocodile that ever lived. *Pachyrachis* was an aquatic reptile that had the long body of a snake and may have been related to the ancestor of today's snakes. All these reptiles were alive during the Cretaceous period, 145 to 65 million years ago.

The line of descent The first known turtles had shells and looked very much like the turtles and tortoises of today. It is thought that today's turtles are direct descendants of the very first reptile group, the anapsids. The anapsids later gave rise to two other groups: the synapsid reptiles, the ancestors of the mammals, and the diapsid reptiles which included the dinosaurs, crocodiles and other archosaurs, the squamates and the rhynchocephalians of which the tuatara is the only living member.

Squamate origins Lizards, snakes and amphisbaenians, which make up the majority of modern reptiles, are squamates. Their ancestors date back at least 200 million years though modern species do not appear until about 20 million years ago. Lizards appeared first, with amphisbaenians and snakes coming later, probably as evolutionary offshoots from lizards.

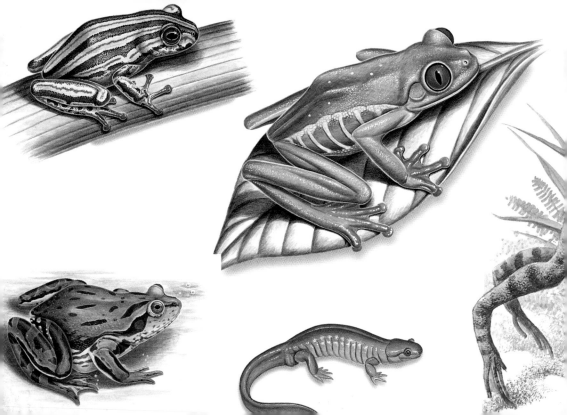

PART TWO

KINDS OF
AMPHIBIANS

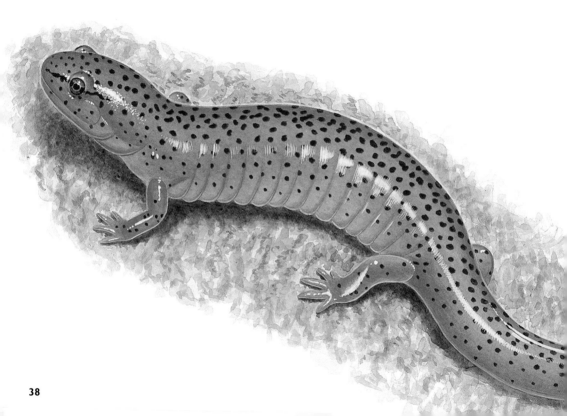

SALAMANDERS
AND
NEWTS

These fascinating creatures have been the subject of countless myths and legends since ancient times. Even today a salamander known as the "white dragon" is revered in eastern China as a god and pilgrimages are made to the pool where it lives. Some of the stories surrounding salamanders and newts may have arisen because they have secretive lifestyles, usually only emerging from their hideaways on mild, damp nights. They look quite different from other amphibians with their long tail and, in most cases, two sets of limbs set at right angles to their elongated body. Superficially they look like lizards, but their complete lack of scales immediately distinguishes them from this group.

HELLBENDERS AND GIANT SALAMANDERS

These solid, bulky animals are the largest of all the salamanders, with the Chinese salamander growing to a length of nearly 6 feet (1.8 m) Hellbenders and giant salamanders never leave the water. They feed mostly at night and spend the day under rocks. They lie in wait for their prey, relying on smell and touch to locate it and catching it with a quick sideways snap of the mouth.

CLASSIFICATION

ORDER CAUDATA
10 FAMILIES • C. 63 GENERA • C. 440 SPECIES
FAMILY CRYPTOBRANCHIDAE

Characteristics Hellbenders and giant salamanders breathe through their lungs but they also have large skin folds along their flanks that increase the surface area through which oxygen can be taken in via their skin from the water. They have small eyes set far back on the sides of their heads and their vision is poor.

Diet They eat virtually any small animal that shares their habitat: worms, insects, crayfish, snails, fish, even smaller salamanders.

Reproduction Each female lays up to 450 eggs, in paired rosary-like strings. Unlike most salamanders, fertilization occurs outside the female's body. The male releases his sperm on the eggs and seems to guard them until they hatch 10 to 12 weeks later.

Habitat Hellbenders, found in the USA, and giant salamanders, found in Japan and China, always live in flowing rivers and streams.

The Japanese giant salamander Andrias japonicus *grows to about 5 feet (1.5 m) in length.*

SIRENS

With their long, slender bodies, small forelimbs and no hindlimbs, sirens look rather eel-like. They are often nocturnal, spending the day burrowed in mud and weeds. Like eels, they can cover short distances on land at night during rainy periods. If their habitat dries out, they can survive for months embedded in the mud, enveloped by a kind of mucous cocoon with only the snout poking out.

CLASSIFICATION

ORDER CAUDATA
10 FAMILIES • C. 63 GENERA • C. 440 SPECIES
FAMILY SIRENIDAE

Characteristics Sirens do not metamorphose so they retain larval structures such as external gills throughout their life. They vary in length from 4 to 35 inches (10–90 cm), depending on the species.

Diet Sirens feed on a variety of invertebrate animals and plants, and the greater siren also eats small fish.

Reproduction Eggs have been found attached to submerged plants, either singly or in small clumps. The female guards the eggs until they hatch. It is not known how fertilization occurs.

Habitat Sirens spend their lives in shallow water in ponds, swamps and ditches which have a muddy bottom and rich aquatic vegetation. They are found in southern USA and Mexico.

The dwarf siren Pseudobranchus striatus of North America is a fully aquatic salamander.

SALAMANDER LIFECYCLES

There is no one lifecycle that applies to all the diverse members of this order. However there are three general types that cover many species: entirely terrestrial, entirely aquatic and, by far the most common, the amphibious lifecycle where the female or both sexes return to the water to breed, usually in the spring.

All aquatic Adults live, mate and lay eggs in the water, usually in large clutches. The eggs hatch into larvae, which also live in the water. Some species do not metamorphose and the adults retain larval structures such as external gills throughout their entire life.

Like all newts, the rough-skinned newt Taricha granulosa has aquatic larvae.

Totally terrestrial Mating takes place on land and the female lays a small number of eggs in a damp place such as a partly rotten log. The entire larval stage of development takes place inside the egg. A miniature version of the adult hatches from the egg. In a few species the female retains the eggs inside her body and gives birth to well-developed larvae or to metamorphosed young.

A bit of both The adults of those salamanders with an amphibious lifecycle spend most of their lives on land but migrate to water to breed. Often quite large clutches of eggs are laid in the water. The larvae metamorphose into juveniles which leave the water to live on land until they are ready to reproduce, a process that takes one to seven years.

THE AMPHIBIOUS LIFECYCLE

Larval development in salamanders varies greatly between species. In the basic amphibious lifecycle, much of the development occurs outside the egg. After a period of time varying from a few days to several years depending on the species, the larva undergoes metamorphosis, losing its external gills and the fins on its back and tail, and changing in other external and internal parts of its body.

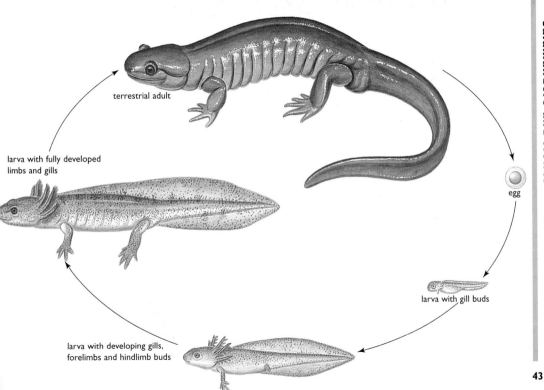

terrestrial adult

larva with fully developed limbs and gills

egg

larva with gill buds

larva with developing gills, forelimbs and hindlimb buds

WATERDOGS AND THE MUDPUPPY

The waterdogs and mudpuppy of North America are totally aquatic. They forage for prey at night and hide themselves under rocks and debris during the day. Their red or purple external gills look like miniature ostrich feathers. These vary in size depending on the oxygen content of the water where they live.

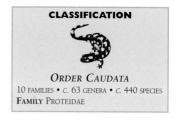

CLASSIFICATION

ORDER CAUDATA
10 FAMILIES • *C.* 63 GENERA • *C.* 440 SPECIES
FAMILY PROTEIDAE

Characteristics All members of the Proteidae family retain their gills. They have large, flat heads, stout bodies, small limbs and usually have a mottled appearance. They vary in length from 9 to 30 inches (22–75 cm).

Diet Mudpuppies and waterdogs feed on a variety of animals including insects, crayfish and fish.

Reproduction A female lays 20–90 eggs, attaching them to the undersides of rocks and logs. They are guarded by the male until they hatch.

Habitat These salamanders live in streams, rivers and lakes, sometimes in running water, sometimes in stagnant, muddy water.

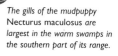

The gills of the mudpuppy Necturus maculosus are largest in the warm swamps in the southern part of its range.

CONGO EELS

If it were not for the presence of four tiny limbs, these large salamanders could easily be mistaken for eels, hence their common name. They live in water and, like eels, burrow into the mud and can move across wet ground. Despite their permanently aquatic lifestyle, congo eels breathe air through lungs by periodically poking their nostrils above the surface of the water. They are active at night when they search for prey.

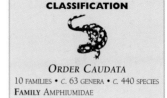

CLASSIFICATION

ORDER CAUDATA
10 FAMILIES • C. 63 GENERA • C. 440 SPECIES
FAMILY AMPHIUMIDAE

Characteristics The adults retain some larval characteristics but lose their external gills. They have long, slender, flexible bodies, sometimes exceeding 3 feet (1 m) in length.

Diet Congo eels feed on crayfish, frogs, fish and small snakes.

Reproduction The eggs are laid in shallow, muddy water under shelters such as a log, in long strings, each containing up to 150 eggs or more. The female coils her body around them until they hatch.

If the water has dried up when they hatch, the young have to find their way to water, usually when it rains.

Habitat Congo eels inhabit swamps, streams, and drainage ditches in southeastern USA, spending much of their time in burrows in the mud.

The three species in the Amphiumidae family have different numbers of toes on their tiny limbs. Amphiuma means is the two-toed species.

MOLE SALAMANDERS

The mole salamanders of North America spend their life almost entirely underground, emerging from their subterranean world only to return to the ponds or streams where they reproduce. In some areas there are members of various species where the adults retain their larval form even when they reach sexual maturity. The most famous of these is the Mexican axolotl.

Characteristics Mole salamanders have broad heads, strong limbs and heavily built, squat bodies, usually less than 14 inches (35 cm) in length. They have smooth, shiny skin and some of them have bright colored markings.

Diet Mole salamanders are carnivorous. Depending on their size, they will eat earthworms, many kinds of insects, spiders,

The tiger salamander Ambystoma tigrinum mavortium is one of the largest terrestrial salamanders.

frogs, tadpoles, and even small snakes and mice.

Reproduction Fertilization, often preceded by a nuptial dance, is immediately followed by the laying of up to 200 eggs. Most species lay their eggs in water attached to submerged objects like logs or roots. Others bury their eggs on land where water will fill the nest when it rains. Only the marbled salamander, which lays its eggs in dry pond beds, has been observed guarding the eggs. She coils herself around them until the rains come.

Habitat Mole salamanders live in burrows or under litter on the forest floor, returning to still ponds and lakes to breed. They are found from southern Alaska and Canada, throughout the USA to most of Mexico.

CLASSIFICATION

ORDER CAUDATA
10 FAMILIES • C. 63 GENERA • C. 440 SPECIES
FAMILY AMBYSTOMATIDAE

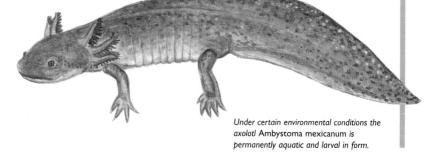

Under certain environmental conditions the axolotl Ambystoma mexicanum *is permanently aquatic and larval in form.*

LUNGLESS SALAMANDERS

This is the largest family of salamanders. As their common name suggests, they have no lungs. Lungless salamanders breathe through their skin and the lining of their mouth. Because their skin must remain moist to absorb oxygen, these animals spend much of their time hidden away in damp places. They shelter in caves, crevices in rocks, spaces between roots and stones, or under logs, and will only venture out when it is humid enough and the temperature is mild, usually on rainy nights.

The red salamander Pseudotriton ruber *is found near brooks and springs in central to eastern North America.*

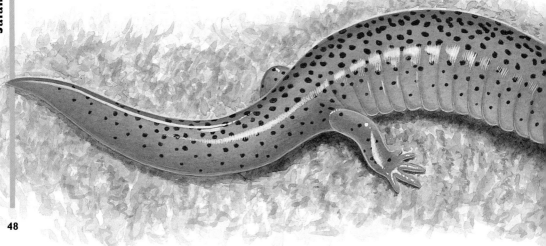

Characteristics Lungless salamanders have long, slender bodies and tails, ranging in length from 1½ to 8 inches (4–20 cm). Their color varies, but many are spotted, mottled or striped. Unlike other salamanders, they have a groove, lined with glands, which runs between the lip and nostril and which transfers chemicals from the salamander's moist environment to sensory receptors inside the nostril which identify those chemicals.

Diet Lungless salamanders feed on a wide variety of invertebrate prey including slugs, snails, worms, beetles, ants, mites and flies.

Reproduction After fertilization, terrestrial species lay their eggs on the ground or on vegetation and the young hatch as miniature adults. Aquatic species lay their eggs in water and the eggs hatch into larvae. In both cases the female guards the eggs.

Habitat Most species are totally terrestrial, occupying a diverse range of damp habitats from burrows and caves to rocks and trees. Others have an aquatic larval stage, and a few are completely aquatic, living in fast-flowing streams. Most species occur in the Americas—from Nova Scotia and British Columbia south to Bolivia and Brazil. A few species are found in France, Sardinia and Italy.

CLASSIFICATION

ORDER CAUDATA
10 FAMILIES • *C.* 63 GENERA • *C.* 440 SPECIES
FAMILY PLETHODONTIDAE

The completely terrestrial yellow-eyed salamander Ensatina eschscholtzii *lives under logs and rocks on the forest floor.*

49

NEWTS AND "TRUE SALAMANDERS"

The term "newt" refers to the members of 10 genera in the Salamandridae family that are partly or entirely aquatic in their adult form. Most newts spend at least half the year in water. Here they court, lay eggs, and build up the fat reserves needed to survive the winter on land. Adults of the rest of the salamanders in the family, the true salamanders, are predominantly or entirely terrestrial. They are secretive animals, usually only active on mild, damp nights.

Characteristics Salamandridae have slender bodies, well-developed limbs, and a long tail that is fin-like in aquatic forms. Their overall length ranges from 3 to 12 inches (7–30 cm). Many have bright and gaudy colors and patterns, warning predators of the poison glands in their skin. Newts, unlike all other salamanders, have rough skin.

Diet Whether they live on land or in water, newts and true salamanders

Newts in the terrestrial phase, like this marbled newt Triturus marmoratus *from Europe, take on the appearance of typical salamanders.*

feed on small invertebrates, including worms, slugs, insects and crustaceans. Some aquatic forms prey on frog tadpoles.

Reproduction Fertilization typically occurs after a long and elaborate courtship. Nearly all the Salamandridae lay eggs in water. Two mountain-dwelling species, the alpine salamander and the fire salamander, give birth to completely metamorphosed young.

Habitat True salamanders live in burrows and under logs and stones in moist woodlands and subalpine meadows. They occur only in Europe with the exception of the fire salamander which is also found in the Middle East and north-west Africa. Newts are more widespread, occurring in Europe, the Middle East, Asia and North America. In their aquatic phase they live in ponds and streams. When on land they live under logs, rocks and dense ground litter.

CLASSIFICATION

ORDER CAUDATA
10 FAMILIES • C. 63 GENERA • C. 440 SPECIES
FAMILY SALAMANDRIDAE

When newts return to ponds in early spring, they regain a number of larval characteristics. This male alpine newt Triturus alpestris *from Europe has developed fin-like extensions on its tail and back.*

STAYING ALIVE

Most salamanders are active at dusk or at night, usually in the warmer seasons. When they emerge from their hiding places to find food, they in turn are preyed upon by other animals. Their predators include other amphibians, turtles, snakes, lizards, fish, birds, mammals and even large beetles, spiders and centipedes.

Surviving the cold When it is too cold or dry, many salamander species take refuge under rotting vegetation or buried rocks, in rock crevices or deep in the ground. Here they remain inactive, often for very long periods, until conditions are suitable again.

Always carnivores Salamanders and newts are all carnivorous and they are carnivorous at all stages in their lifecycles. Usually they feed on small invertebrates such as insects, spiders, crustaceans, mollusks and worms. The larger species also prey on small vertebrates, such as small fish, and cannibalism can occur in both larvae and adults. Salamanders usually snap up their catch with their mouth and some can flick their tongue quite a distance forward to catch small prey.

Defense When in danger, salamanders defend themselves by secreting toxic or sticky substances. Some have the glands that produce these unpalatable secretions on the back of their neck. The spotted

LOST BY A TAIL

This red-backed salamander, from the lungless salamander family, is about to become dinner for the ring-neck snake. If the snake had caught the unlucky salamander by the tail it may have been able to escape as lungless salamanders are able to shed their tail and grow a new one.

Salamanders prey mainly on small invertebrates. This spotted salamander a species from the mole salamander family, investigates a worm.

salamander, for example, bends its head down or holds it flat against the ground when attacked, thus presenting the attacker with the most distasteful part of its body. Some mole salamanders actually head butt their enemies. Other salamanders, such as the newts, assume a rigid posture that displays their brightly colored undersides, a warning to would-be predators that their skin is toxic. One posture, known as the unken reflex, involves arching the body with the tail perpendicular to it (or sometimes rolled up) to reveal the brightly colored underside of the tail and body.

Making a noise Unlike frogs and toads, salamanders do not usually make sounds as they have no larynx, or only a rudimentary one, and no vocal chords. However, if disturbed or excited, the fire salamander and some newts can produce a weak squeak and the sirens give a faint yelp.

CAECILIANS

Caecilians are long, worm-like, mostly secretive, burrowing creatures which are found only in the tropical and subtropical regions of the world. They are the only living amphibians that are completely legless. Although their name (pronounced "see-sil-e-an") means "blind," most caecilians have small eyes, which in some species are hidden below the bones of the skull. Caecilians are the least known of the three orders of amphibians. They rarely emerge from their burrows so they are very difficult to find and observe. Caecilians are so little known, in fact, that most of them, like *Ichthyophis kohtaoensis* (left) of South-East Asia, have no common name.

CAECILIANS

Caecilians are capable of moving snake-like across land when forced to do so, but normally they live underground. They move through existing tunnels or create new ones by pushing their head through moist soil or loose mud. Even the most aquatic species are adept at burrowing into the soft mud and gravel on the bottoms and edges of the streams and rivers where they live.

Dermophis mexicanus *of Mexico and Central America is a terrestrial species that grows to more than 2 feet (60 cm).*

Characteristics The caecilians vary in length from a tiny 3 inches (7 cm) to nearly 5 feet (1.5 m). They have numerous skin folds, or rings, that partially or completely encircle their body. Terrestrial caecilians have a cylindrical body. Aquatic and semi-aquatic species are flattened from side to side and have a fin running the length of their back to facilitate movement through water.

Caecilians have smooth skin which, like all amphibians, contains numerous poison glands. Most species are subdued in color, usually shades of bluish gray, but some are boldly colored and marked, perhaps as a warning to predators of their poisonous skin secretions. Caecilians move by undulating their bodies, with the muscle action going from the head to the back. They have a unique pair of sensory organs, called tentacles, which emerge from a groove on each side of the snout between the eye and the nostril. The tentacles, probably organs of taste and/or smell, are admirably suited for sensing the environment of tunnels.

Diet All caecilians are carnivorous. Land-dwelling species seem to feed primarily on earthworms. They also eat beetles and other insects, and occasionally small frogs and lizards. Aquatic species eat insects, earthworms and other invertebrates. When caecilians locate prey, they approach it slowly and seize it with their jaws.

Reproduction Unlike most other amphibians, all caecilians have internal fertilization. Some species lay eggs that hatch into water-dwelling larvae which later metamorphose into adults. Some lay eggs that hatch directly into terrestrial juveniles with no larval stage. Other species give birth to live young, again with no larval stage. Females of the egg-laying species remain with their eggs until they hatch.

Habitat Terrestrial caecilians live in moist soil, leaf litter and rotten logs in tropical forested areas. Aquatic species live in rivers and streams and aquatic larvae live in seepages and streams. Caecilians are found in Central and South America, South-East Asia, India, the Seychelles archipelago in the Indian Ocean, and in equatorial Africa.

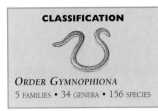

CLASSIFICATION

ORDER GYMNOPHIONA
5 FAMILIES • 34 GENERA • 156 SPECIES

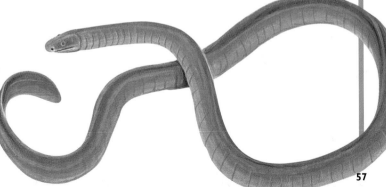

Typhlonectes natans *is an aquatic caecilian from South America which gives birth to fully developed young.*

BUILT FOR BURROWING

The caecilian skull is powerfully constructed with a pointed snout and an underslung lower jaw or recessed mouth, features that allow the head to be used as a ram to push through soil or mud. This is just one of the many adaptations the caecilians have for burrowing.

Rod and tube The body muscles of caecilians are arranged so the body can act like a rod moving within a tube. The "tube" is the skin and outer layer of body muscles. The "rod" is the head, backbone and the muscles attached to the backbone. With the tube fixed in position in a tunnel, the rod can be pushed slightly forward through the soil to extend the tunnel. When the tip of the rod—the head—has gone as far forward as it can, the tube is pulled forward and fixed in position so the rod can again be pushed through the soil.

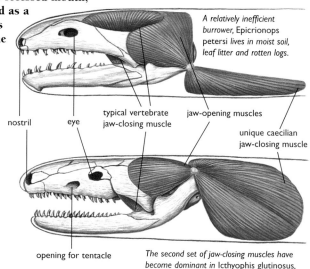

A relatively inefficient burrower, Epicrionops petersi lives in moist soil, leaf litter and rotten logs.

nostril · eye · typical vertebrate jaw-closing muscle · jaw-opening muscles · unique caecilian jaw-closing muscle

opening for tentacle

The second set of jaw-closing muscles have become dominant in Icthyophis glutinosus, a proficient burrower.

A small terrestrial burrower from Venezuela, Microcaecilia rabei grows to only about 8 inches (20 cm).

nostril
opening for tentacle
typical vertebrate jaw-closing muscle
jaw-opening muscle
unique caecilian jaw-closing muscle

The totally terrestrial Crotaphatrema lamottei has a deeply recessed mouth.

Jaw muscles Typical vertebrates have a single set of jaw-closing muscles that pull on the lower jaw from a point in front of the jaw hinge. Caecilians have these muscles, too, but they are the only vertebrates with a second set of jaw-closing muscles. These help close the jaw by pulling back and down on a special extension behind the lower jaw hinge in much the same way as pushing down one end of a seesaw causes the other end to swing up. These muscles improve burrowing efficiency.

BETTER BURROWERS

Some caecilian species are better burrowers than others. The more efficient burrowers make more use of the second set of muscles, reflected by the increased muscle size shown in the illustrations. They also have more rigid skulls and their mouth is more recessed.

Kinds of Amphibians
FROGS AND TOADS

When the words "frog" and "toad" were coined, they were used to distinguish two common European amphibians: the frog, now known as *Rana temporaria*, a smooth-skinned, long-legged creature that jumps, and the toad, now known as *Bufo bufo*, a warty, short-legged creature that walks. When new species were found in other parts of the world they were named "frog" or "toad" according to their superficial resemblance to the "first" frog or toad. However this distinction was not scientific and began to break down where species were more diverse. "Frog" may be used for any anuran, whereas "toad" is used for members of the genus *Bufo* as well as for other frogs of similar body form.

TAILED FROG

The tailed frog *Ascaphus truei* does not have a true tail but rather a small appendage, present only in the male, which is adapted to insert sperm directly into the female. This ensures that the sperm is not washed away in the rapidly flowing water where the frogs mate and makes it one of the few frogs to have internal fertilization. It is most active at night around the streams where it lives.

CLASSIFICATION

ORDER ANURA
28 FAMILIES
C. 338 GENERA • C. 4,360 SPECIES
FAMILY ASCAPHIDAE

Characteristics The tailed frog has a slender body, slightly webbed toes, and varies in length from 1 to 3 inches (3–7 cm).

Diet The frog eats insects and other invertebrates. The tadpoles eat algae.

Reproduction The eggs are attached to the undersides of rocks in water. Tadpoles take three years to develop. They have large suckers on their mouths which they use to cling onto rocks while feeding.

Habitat The tailed frog is semi-aquatic, living in and around cold, fast-flowing mountain streams in north-western USA and in south-western Canada.

Painted Frogs

Painted frogs are usually found at the edges and in the shallows of streams, lakes and ponds. Often they can be seen sitting in shallow pools with their head just above the surface of the water. On land they shelter under logs or in rocky crevices. They are usually active at night but some are also active during the day.

Characteristics Some species have quite plump bodies, but others are slender. They range in size from 2 to 3 inches (5–7 cm). Their color patterns are often highly variable.

Diet Painted frogs eat a wide variety of insects, spiders and other invertebrates.

Reproduction The eggs are laid in water and the tadpoles are aquatic.

Habitat The frogs live near ponds, streams or lakes or in woodlands and rocky areas. They are found in western Europe, the Middle East and northwest Africa.

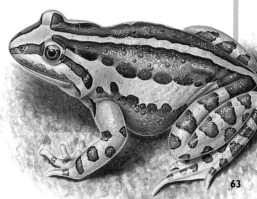

The European painted frog Discoglossus pictus *cannot extend its tongue to catch prey so instead lunges forward and grabs it with its mouth.*

63

FIRE-BELLIED TOADS

These largely aquatic toads are small and warty-skinned with colorful red, orange or yellow undersides. When they are disturbed they arch their back and throw up their arms and legs thus revealing their bright belly and warning predators that their skin secretions are distasteful and mildly toxic. Sometimes they expose their belly by turning over onto their back.

CLASSIFICATION

ORDER ANURA
28 FAMILIES
C. 338 GENERA • C. 4,360 SPECIES
FAMILY BOMINATORIDAE

Characteristics Fire-bellied toads have a flattened body, a disk-shaped tongue, and are 1 to 3 inches (3–7 cm) in length. They have an unusual call, producing it during the inhaled breath rather than on the exhalation like most frogs.

The brightly colored underside of the Oriental fire-bellied toad Bombina orientalis *warns of its mildly toxic, unpalatable skin secretion.*

Diet The toads eat worms, small crustaceans and other invertebrates. They catch flying insects that land on the water's surface or fly just above it.

Reproduction The eggs are large and are laid either singly at the bottom of ponds, or in groups, often attached to aquatic plants.

Habitat The toads usually inhabit shallow water at the edges of rivers, streams, marshes, drainage ditches and in temporary puddles. They are found in Europe and Asia.

MEXICAN BURROWING TOAD

A rather strange looking creature, the Mexican burrowing toad *Rhinophrynus dorsalis* spends most of its life underground, emerging only to breed after heavy rain. On the inner edge of each hind foot is a "spade" which the frog uses to dig as it shuffles backward into the earth. When frightened or calling it becomes so inflated with air that it looks almost like a balloon, or a "bag of bones" as one early naturalist described it.

CLASSIFICATION

ORDER ANURA
28 FAMILIES
C. 338 GENERA • C. 4,360 SPECIES
FAMILY RHINOPHRYNIDAE

Characteristics About 3 inches (7 cm) long, the toad has a rotund, oval-shaped body with a pointed snout and short legs. Its tongue projects straight out of its mouth instead of flipping over itself as in most frogs. Its bright colors are unusual for a burrowing frog.

Diet The frog feeds almost exclusively on ants and termites, licking them up with its tongue. The tadpoles are filter feeders; they eat small particles suspended in water.

Reproduction Many eggs are laid in temporary ponds caused by heavy rains. The tadpoles hatch after a few days and take one to three months to change into adults.

Habitat
The Mexican burrowing toad is found in drier lowland areas ranging from southern Texas to Costa Rica.

AFRICAN CLAWED FROGS

These are the frogs once used to test for pregnancy—a female injected with the urine of a pregnant woman spontaneously lays eggs. The frogs rarely, if ever, venture out of water. Along with the other members of the Pipidae family, they have no tongue but rely heavily on their hands to capture food. They hang just below the surface of the water, arms outstretched, waiting for prey to swim by, or they unearth it with the claws on their feet and scoop it up with their long fingers.

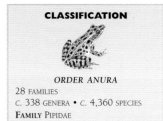

CLASSIFICATION

ORDER ANURA

28 FAMILIES
C. 338 GENERA • C. 4,360 SPECIES
FAMILY PIPIDAE

Characteristics The frogs have flattened bodies, powerful legs, and large fully webbed feet with claw-like structures on three toes.

The Cape clawed frog Xenopus gilli has black horny caps on three of the toes on its hind feet.

Diet Arthropods are the main part of the frogs' diet but they also eat fish and other amphibians. Tadpoles filter the protozoan-rich mud.

Reproduction Unlike most frogs, courtship is a quiet affair, its call being a faint chirping made under water. The eggs are laid singly and may be attached to aquatic plants, rocks or debris.

Habitat Clawed frogs live in ponds, rivers and stagnant pools in Africa, south of the Sahara Desert.

SURINAM TOAD

Built like a squared-off pancake with a limb at each corner, the almost entirely aquatic Surinam toad *Pipa pipa* is one of the more bizarre tropical frogs. Its breeding behavior is equally bizarre. The male distributes the eggs over the female's back where they sink into spongy tissue. The skin swells up around the eggs and within a day or two each egg is embedded in an individual pocket. Here they develop into tiny, fully formed froglets.

CLASSIFICATION

ORDER ANURA
28 FAMILIES
c. 338 GENERA • *c.* 4,360 SPECIES
FAMILY PIPIDAE

Characteristics The Surinam toad has large, fully webbed feet and powerful hindlimbs. Its flat head has a pointed beak and tiny, lidless black eyes. It has no tongue but uses its sensitive fingers to capture prey.

Diet The Surinam toad pushes through the detritus and mud on the bottom of streams and lakes, stirring up the worms, insect larvae and other bottom-dwelling invertebrates on which it feeds.

Reproduction The female lays about 100 eggs in a single clutch and carries them on her back for three months. When they are fully developed the froglets swim away.

Habitat The Surinam toad lives in swamps, streams, lakes and other water bodies in South America.

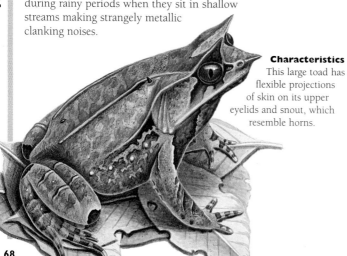

ASIAN HORNED TOAD

The bizarre shape of the Asian horned toad *Megophrys nasuta* and its coloration provide excellent camouflage for its life among the leaf litter on the rainforest floor. With its ribbed, mottled brown skin it looks like a dead leaf and is almost invisible on the forest floor. The males become more noticeable during rainy periods when they sit in shallow streams making strangely metallic clanking noises.

CLASSIFICATION

ORDER ANURA

28 FAMILIES
c. 338 GENERA • c. 4,360 SPECIES
FAMILY MEGOPHRYIDAE

Characteristics
This large toad has flexible projections of skin on its upper eyelids and snout, which resemble horns.

Diet Well camouflaged among the leaf litter, the toad lies in wait for large prey such as rodents and smaller frogs. Tadpoles feed from the water's surface with funnel-shaped mouths.

Reproduction The eggs are laid in water, but little else is known of its reproductive habits.

Habitat The Asian horned toad lives among the leaf litter on the floors of rainforests near rivers and streams in Southeast Asia.

SPADEFOOT TOADS

Spadefoots get their common name from the prominent digging tubercle they have on each hind foot. They use this to dig rapidly backward, circling as they descend. They spend the day and long, dry periods—most of the year if rain is scarce—in their deep, almost vertical burrows. On warm moist nights they may come out to eat, and when it rains they emerge to breed in temporary pools.

CLASSIFICATION

ORDER ANURA
28 FAMILIES
C. 338 GENERA • C. 4,360 SPECIES
FAMILY PELOBATIDAE

Characteristics Spadefoots are plump frogs, up to 4 inches (10 cm) long, with short limbs and large eyes.

Diet The spadefoots eat almost any terrestrial arthropod. The rains that call them out also bring forth hordes of insects, and the frogs can get enough food in a few nights to survive months underground. The tadpoles eat algae and other plant material, while some cannibalize their pond mates.

Reproduction The tadpoles have to develop quickly before the breeding pools dry up. Egg laying to metamorphosis can take less that two weeks.

Habitat Most live in dry areas with sandy soils. They are found in North America, Europe, north-west Africa and western Asia.

Couch's spadefoot Scaphiopus couchii *is a spadefoot toad from North America.*

FROM EGG TO FROG

About three-quarters of the world's frogs and toads have a life history in which eggs laid in water hatch into tadpoles that grow and metamorphose into adult frogs. Within each of these stages many variations occur, and many species do not have free-living tadpoles but lay eggs that hatch into froglets.

Mating Almost all frogs fertilize their eggs externally. The male approaches the female from behind and grasps her around the body with his arms. The frogs maintain this posture until the female expels the eggs and the male releases his sperm onto them.

The eggs Eggs deposited in water are usually grouped in globular masses containing a few to hundreds or thousands of eggs. In still water, the eggs are likely to be spread in a single layer on the surface, and in fast-flowing streams the eggs may be attached singly to submerged rocks.

At about 6 weeks metamorphosis is complete. The young frog leaves the water, switching from a vegetarian diet to one of mainly insects. It lives at the water's edge until it is time to hibernate.

A COMMON LIFE

Like many frogs of the temperate zone, the European common frog *Rana temporaria* comes out of its winter hibernation and migrates to a pond to breed in early spring. The frogs lay their eggs in large communal masses, a behavior that may reduce losses during cold weather.

The lungs become functional and the gills disappear after about 3 weeks. After 4 weeks the tail begins to shrink as the limbs gradually appear.

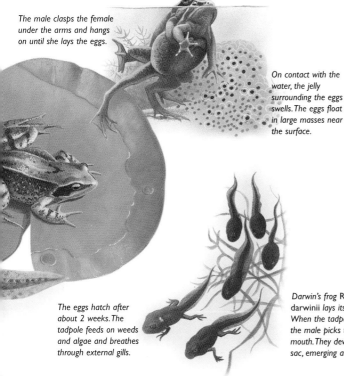

The male clasps the female under the arms and hangs on until she lays the eggs.

On contact with the water, the jelly surrounding the eggs swells. The eggs float in large masses near the surface.

The eggs hatch after about 2 weeks. The tadpole feeds on weeds and algae and breathes through external gills.

Larval life The tadpole stage may be as brief as a week in species breeding in desert rain pools, or up to two years or more, but generally it averages a few weeks. A typical tadpole lives in water, has a strong finned tail and no clear distinction between head and body. The mouth has a beak and rows of "teeth."

All in the egg The species that omit the free-living tadpole stage lay large eggs in moist places such as a rotting log, a burrow, or in a plant that collects water. Development takes place entirely inside the egg which hatches into a fully metamorphosed froglet. In a few species the eggs stay in the female's oviduct where they develop before the froglets are born.

Darwin's frog Rhinoderma darwinii lays its eggs on land. When the tadpoles hatch, the male picks them up in his mouth. They develop in his vocal sac, emerging as small froglets.

BARKING FROG

The barking frog *Eleutherodactylus augusti* has earned its common name from the noise it makes—a short, sharp throaty sound uttered every two or three seconds which resembles the barking of a dog. It is a secretive, ground-dwelling frog, often hiding by day in damp limestone caves and crevices or down mines and wells. When threatened it inflates its body with air so it becomes several times its normal size.

CLASSIFICATION

ORDER ANURA
28 FAMILIES
C. 338 GENERA • C. 4,360 SPECIES
FAMILY LEPTODACTYLIDAE

Characteristics The frog is around 3 inches (7 cm) in length, with the males much smaller than the females. It has a toad-shaped body, a large head and slender, unwebbed toes. It walks rather stiffly with its body and heels held high off the ground.

Diet The barking frog eats insects and other invertebrates.

Reproduction Small clusters of eggs are laid under rocks and logs. Metamorphosis takes place entirely within the egg.

Habitat The frog inhabits rainy limestone areas in south-western North America and Mexico.

ORNATE HORNED TOAD

The ornate horned toad *Ceratophrys ornata* has been called a "mouth with legs" because of its enormous, wide mouth. The toad is a robust, aggressive predator with a big appetite, and it will attack an animal many times its own size. It cannot move quickly, so lies partially buried among leaf litter on the forest floor and ambushes its prey. The toad usually lives in tropical rainforests but its range extends to more arid areas where it will estivate in mud or clay during the dry season.

CLASSIFICATION

ORDER ANURA
28 FAMILIES
C. 338 GENERA • C. 4,360 SPECIES
FAMILY LEPTODACTYLIDAE

Characteristics This large toad is about 8 inches (20 cm) in length and is almost as wide as it is long. Its common name comes from the folds of skin over its eye which resemble small horns.

Diet The ornate horned toad eats almost anything it can swallow: insects, frogs, lizards, even small mammals, small birds and snakes.

Reproduction Small clusters of eggs are laid hidden under rocks and logs.

Habitat The ornate horned toad lives in tropical rainforests in Argentina. It can also survive in more arid regions.

SOUTH AMERICAN BULLFROG

Like some other members of the genus, the South American bullfrog *Leptodactylus pentadactylus* is a very large frog that is often eaten by humans. In the West Indies the meat of the hind legs is served up as "mountain chicken." Because of its value as a food source to humans and others, really large examples are not plentiful.

CLASSIFICATION

ORDER ANURA
28 FAMILIES
C. 338 GENERA • C. 4,360 SPECIES
FAMILY LEPTODACTYLIDAE

Characteristics The South American bullfrog is a large and chunky frog, growing to 8 inches (20 cm). During the breeding season its legs turn a deep red or orange in contrast with the dark brown or green of the rest of its body. The male has a prominent black spur on its thumb and others on its breast to assist in holding the female during mating.

Diet A variety of small invertebrates form this species' diet.

Reproduction This species lays its eggs in foam "nests" which are constructed while the frogs mate. The male uses his feet to whip the mixture of eggs and seminal fluid into a froth. The nest protects the fertilized eggs, and then the tadpoles, from enemies.

Habitat As its common name suggests, this frog is distributed over most of South and Central America.

GOLD FROG

This tiny frog, named for its bright golden yellow color, builds burrows among the leaf litter on the forest floor of its restricted Brazilian habitat. On its back the gold frog *Brachycephalus ephippium* has a peculiar, cross-shaped bony shield that is fused to its backbone. This shield is probably used to plug the entrance to its burrow.

CLASSIFICATION

ORDER ANURA
28 FAMILIES
C. 338 GENERA •C. 4,360 SPECIES
FAMILY BRACHYCEPHALIDAE

Characteristics These are small frogs, with a body length of less than half an inch (1.2 cm) and greatly reduced phalanges. They have only three functional toes on each foot and two on the hand. The horizontal pupil is remarkably large for such a diminutive frog

Diet Little is known about the food preferences of this tiny species.

Reproduction A small number of large eggs are laid on land. Direct development takes place in the eggs, which hatch into tiny froglets, omitting the tadpole stage.

Habitat The gold frog lives in the humid coastal region of south-eastern Brazil.

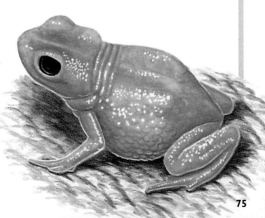

SPOTTED GRASS FROG

The semi-aquatic spotted grass frog *Limnodynastes tasmaniensis* is usually found in marshy, wet areas or near streams and ponds with grassy edges. During the day it sits under stones, fallen timber and debris close to the water's edge. In hot, dry periods it shelters in cracks in the ground, usually under large rocks, where temperatures are lower.

CLASSIFICATION

ORDER ANURA

28 FAMILIES
C. 338 GENERA • C. 4,360 SPECIES
FAMILY MYOBATRACHIDAE

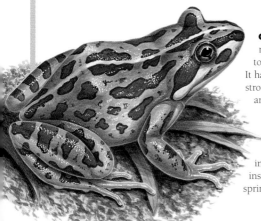

Characteristics This medium-sized frog grows to about 2 inches (5 cm). It has a pointed head, strong limbs and its toes are slightly webbed.

Diet The spotted grass frog eats a wide range of small invertebrates including insects, spiders, worms and springtails.

Reproduction The eggs are laid in a white foamy mass on the surface of still water. They are usually attached to vegetation and exposed to sunlight.

Habitat The spotted grass frog lives near streams, ponds, marshes and other temporary water in woodlands, shrublands and grasslands. It is widespread in eastern Australia and has also been seen in Western Australia.

CORROBOREE FROG

The vivid coloration of the tiny corroboree frog *Pseudophryne corroboree* is similar to the striped ocher and charcoal decorations which the Aboriginal people of Australia paint on their bodies for ceremonial dances, or corroborees. Although its skin is toxic, it is thought that the bright colors are also useful in deterring predators.

CLASSIFICATION

ORDER ANURA
28 FAMILIES
C. 338 GENERA • C. 4,360 SPECIES
FAMILY MYOBATRACHIDAE

Characteristics This small, squat frog grows to a little over an inch (3 cm) long. It has a rather toad-like gait, walking slowly on its short limbs and making occasional short leaps.

Diet Ants are the main part of this frog's diet but it also eats other small invertebrates.

Reproduction The female lays about 12 eggs in a burrow in sphagnum moss. The tadpoles hatch when rain floods the nest in winter or when the snow melts in spring. If conditions are not wet enough, hatching is delayed.

Habitat The corroboree frog lives in burrows in damp places such as bogs, seepages and marshes. It is found at altitudes above 5,000 feet (1,500 m) in the Australian Alps in New South Wales. Its numbers have declined dramatically in recent years.

CRUCIFIX TOAD

The crucifix toad *Notaden bennetti* is well adapted to life in dry areas where rainfall is sparse and seasonal. It spends much of its time buried underground and is seldom seen or heard except when it emerges to mate, feed and breed after heavy rain. When threatened it rises on all fours and puffs out its body to an absurd size. It secretes a thick, yellow toxin when disturbed, so it is likely that its bright colors serve as a warning to enemies.

CLASSIFICATION

ORDER ANURA
28 FAMILIES
C. 338 GENERA • C. 4,360 SPECIES
FAMILY MYOBATRACHIDAE

Characteristics This medium-sized, squat, short-legged frog has warty skin, a blunt snout and grows to about 2 inches (5 cm). It has a spade on each hind foot. that it uses to dig backward into loose soil.

Diet The crucifix toad eats only ants and termites.

Reproduction The toad spawns in temporary pools caused by heavy rain. The tadpoles have to develop quickly before the water evaporates, usually within two or three weeks.

Habitat These Australian toads inhabit the semi-arid slopes and plains west of the Great Dividing Range in southern Queensland and New South Wales, especially the black soils of inland river floodplains.

LEOPARD TOAD

With its dry warty skin, short limbs and large parotid (toxin-producing) glands behind the eyes, the strikingly marked leopard toad *Bufo pardalis* is a typical true toad. Like all members of the *Bufo* genus, the leopard toad is a ground dweller which hides during the day, usually in holes, and emerges at night to hop about looking for prey which it snaps up with its long sticky tongue.

CLASSIFICATION

ORDER ANURA
28 FAMILIES • C. 338 GENERA •
C. 4,360 SPECIES
FAMILY BUFONIDAE

Characteristics This is sometimes called the snoring toad because of its deep, pulsating snoring sound. It makes one call every three or four seconds. Its distinctive warty back is symmetrically patched; the underside is whitish.

Diet The leopard toad usually feeds on small invertebrates.

Reproduction Huge numbers of eggs are laid in paired strings in permanent water such as dams or waterholes. The jelly surrounding the eggs is quite distasteful, thus discouraging fish and other animals from eating them.

Habitat The leopard toad prefers deep waterholes, dams and other watery habitats. It is a native of southern Africa.

ASIATIC CLIMBING TOAD

The tree-dwelling Asiatic climbing toad *Pedostibes hosii* is well adapted to its arboreal lifestyle, with long limbs and broad adhesive pads on the digits that enable the toad to grip slippery leaves and branches. Males are brown or blackish above with distinct bars or crossbars on the limbs. Females are purplish in color, with bright yellow spots, or olive green with chrome yellow spots on the sides and beneath.

CLASSIFICATION

ORDER ANURA

28 FAMILIES
C. 338 GENERA • C. 4,360 SPECIES
FAMILY BUFONIDAE

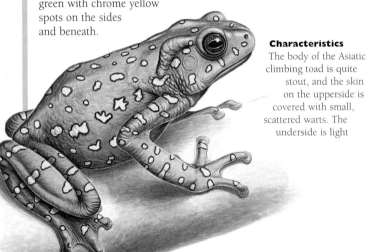

Characteristics

The body of the Asiatic climbing toad is quite stout, and the skin on the upperside is covered with small, scattered warts. The underside is light and finely granular. Males grow to 3 inches (7 cm) and females can be an inch longer.

Diet Small invertebrates are the favored food.

Reproduction Little is known of its reproductive biology, although it lays large numbers of eggs.

Habitat This species lives in Asian rainforests, usually well hidden in bushes and small trees in the dense parts of the forest.

VARIABLE HARLEQUIN FROG

Looking more like the unrelated poison frogs than its relatives the toads, the variable harlequin frog *Atelopus varius* of South and Central America is brilliantly colored, a clear warning that its skin secretes potent toxins. As the variable harlequin frog is slow moving and active during the day, this warning is probably a powerful deterrent to help fend off potential predators.

CLASSIFICATION

ORDER ANURA
28 FAMILIES
C. 338 GENERA • C. 4,360 SPECIES
FAMILY BUFONIDAE

Characteristics The strong colors of this frog are its most distinctive feature, and its common name is apt, for it resembles the bright hues of a circus harlequin. The front digits are elongated to enable better purchase.

Diet Like other toads, this species feeds on small invertebrates.

Reproduction Large, unpigmented eggs are laid in fast-flowing streams. The tadpoles have sucker-like mouths as well as an adhesive disk on their abdomen so they can stay put while feeding.

Habitat There are 43 species of *Atelopus,* and they are wide-ranging in distribution from Costa Rica to Bolivia, the Guianan region and coastal eastern Brazil.

PREDATORS AND PREY

All frogs are carnivores and many are not fussy feeders but will eat whatever small animals share their habitat and fit into their huge mouths. In turn, frogs are preyed upon by a host of enemies, ranging from tarantulas to birds to humans. The larval stage, too, is a perilous time. Almost any meat-eater will find a tadpole a succulent morsel.

Some invertebrates eat frogs. This leopard frog has been captured by a giant water bug.

What frogs eat Relatively few frogs are large enough to eat other vertebrates, so most of them eat insects and other arthropods, and earthworms. Some of the larger frogs, such as the North American bullfrog, can take birds and mice, small turtles and fish, young snakes, and, in crowded conditions, smaller frogs of their own and other species.

What tadpoles eat Tadpoles for the most part are vegetarian. They filter organisms from the water, scrape algae from rocks and stones, and consume bottom debris. Some scavenge on the carcasses of dead animals and other species have predatory tadpoles that capture invertebrates and other tadpoles.

Catching food Most frogs simply sit and wait for prey to come within reach. Some species ambush their

Many snakes live largely or entirely on frogs. This garter snake has just caught an American toad.

A leopard frog devours an earthworm.

prey from hiding places. A few heavy-bodied frogs, such as the South American horned frogs, lure agile prey by waving the long toes on their hind feet. Other frogs, especially the small poison frogs of tropical America, actively forage for small insects among the leaf litter by day. In most frogs, the tongue is attached to the front of the mouth. It can be flicked forward and some distance with considerable speed, snapping up prey with the aid of sticky mucus secreted from glands in the tongue. Frogs that cannot extend their tongue simply lunge forward and grab prey with their mouth, sometimes using their hands to help.

Defense Frogs have many enemies including snakes, wading birds, bats, turtles, crocodilians, spiders, fish and other frogs. Staying hidden is one method of avoiding danger—a camouflaged, motionless frog is very hard to spot. Flight is another—with one or two great bounds on their

A large bullfrog makes a meal of the smaller carpenter frog.

long, powerful hindlimbs a frog can elude an enemy. Sometimes, though, an enemy has to be faced and other defenses are necessary. These include toxic or distasteful skin secretions, feigning death, or puffing up the body to make it look larger. A few South American frogs have brightly colored eyespots on their rump which they display to deter an attacker. There are even some large frogs that actually leap at predators and snap at them.

GREEN AND GOLDEN BELL FROG

The semi-aquatic green and golden bell frog *Litoria aurea* is usually found among bullrushes and reeds either in or near the edge of permanent water. Active at night and during the day, it enjoys basking in the sun, slipping into the water to cool off when necessary. It is a voracious feeder and catches its prey by lunging forward and seizing it with both hands.

CLASSIFICATION

ORDER ANURA
28 FAMILIES • *C.* 338 GENERA •
C. 4,360 SPECIES
FAMILY HYLIDAE

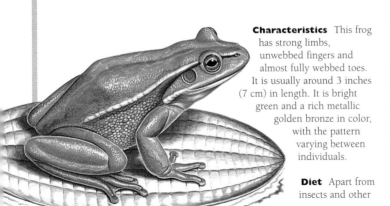

Characteristics This frog has strong limbs, unwebbed fingers and almost fully webbed toes. It is usually around 3 inches (7 cm) in length. It is bright green and a rich metallic golden bronze in color, with the pattern varying between individuals.

Diet Apart from insects and other invertebrates, the frog will eat its own species and has been known to catch small tiger snakes.

Reproduction A loose mass of eggs is deposited among vegetation floating in water. The eggs hatch within a few days and the tadpoles metamorphose about four to six weeks later.

Habitat The frog can be found in streams, swamps, lagoons, ponds and dams in south-eastern Australia.

GIANT TREE FROG

The giant tree frog *Litoria infrafrenata* is one of the world's largest tree frogs and Australia's largest frog. Like all the tree-dwelling members of the Hylidae family, it is a long-legged, powerful jumper. It is fond of human habitation and can often be found on eaves, windows, sheds and inside houses near its habitat. It is particularly active on warm, humid nights when it can be seen catching insects that are attracted to lights.

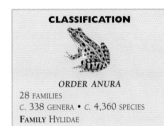

CLASSIFICATION

ORDER ANURA
28 FAMILIES
C. 338 GENERA • C. 4,360 SPECIES
FAMILY HYLIDAE

Characteristics The giant tree frog averages about 4 inches (10 cm) in length, but some individuals reach over 5 inches (14 cm). Broad adhesive pads on its fingers and toes enable it to balance on flimsy leaves. The color can vary in the same individual from pale pinkish fawn to almost black, but it is usually a bright emerald green.

Diet The frog feeds mainly on insects such as beetles and moths but sometimes it eats small mammals such as mice.

Reproduction Breeding takes place in shady swamps where the female lays an egg mass, containing around 400 eggs, in still water. The eggs hatch in a few days and the tadpoles take about eight weeks to metamorphose.

Habitat The giant tree frog lives in damp and humid rainforest areas in north-eastern Australia, New Guinea and surrounding islands. It is also found in eastern Indonesia.

BURROWING TREE FROG

Despite being a member of the tree frog family, the burrowing tree frog *Pternohyla fadiens* does not live in trees but spends much of its life underground. Burrowing tree frogs are nocturnal and rarely seen except when the summer rains bring them out to chorus and mate around the pools. During periods of drought the frog estivates under the surface, forming a cocoon that protects it from drying out.

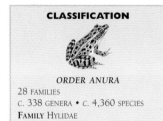

CLASSIFICATION

ORDER ANURA
28 FAMILIES
C. 338 GENERA • C. 4,360 SPECIES
FAMILY HYLIDAE

Characteristics A small frog, it grows to 1 to 2 inches (3–5 cm) in length. It has a shovel-shaped head for burrowing and the skin is fused to its hard, bony skull. It is thought that this bony section might be used to plug the burrow, keeping predators out and moisture in. Unlike other tree frogs, it has no toe pads, but on each hind foot it has a large spade.

Diet The burrowing tree frog eats insects and other small invertebrates.

Reproduction Little is known about the reproductive biology of this elusive species.

Habitat The frog lives down moist burrows in open grasslands in the arid regions of south-western USA and Mexico.

GRAY TREE FROG

With skin that resembles lichen, the gray tree frog *Hyla versicolor* is beautifully camouflaged when it rests on a tree. This and its ability to stay perfectly still for hours at a time provide excellent protection. If an enemy gets too close and the frog decides to flee, it has orange "flash" markings on its groin which only become visible when it leaps away, thus startling and confusing a predator.

CLASSIFICATION

ORDER ANURA
28 FAMILIES
C. 338 GENERA • C. 4,360 SPECIES
FAMILY HYLIDAE

Characteristics About 2 inches (5 cm) in length, the gray tree frog has a short broad head and a stout body. It has large adhesive pads on its fingers and toes.

Diet The gray tree frog eats the insects that share its tree habitat: for example, caterpillars, flies, beetles, ants and tree crickets.

Reproduction The frogs mate after their winter hibernation. The eggs are attached in small groups or singly to grass or plant stems near the surface of the water in ponds or rivers. About seven weeks after the eggs are laid the tadpoles complete metamorphosis and leave the water.

Habitat The frog lives on trees such as gray birch, oak or apple trees. It is very common in eastern North America and can be found around houses on mossy or lichen-covered ledges or posts.

The gray tree frog is perfectly camouflaged as it waits in a tree for potential prey to pass by.

RED-EYED TREE FROG

Except for its vertical pupils, the red-eyed tree frog *Agalychnis callidryas* is a typical tree-dwelling hylid. The end of each finger and toe is expanded into a specialized pad which allows the frog to stick to vertical surfaces. Its long limbs and slender body allow it to leap from one leaf or branch to another and to hold onto its perch.

A LARGE FAMILY
There are more than 770 species of tree frogs in the Hylidae family, in 40 genera. More than 500 of these, including the red-eyed tree frog, live in the Americas, especially the tropical regions of Central and South America. Most species are arboreal or climbing forms.

Characteristics The red-eyed tree frogs share adaptations common to most tree frogs, with specialized adhesive pads, long limbs and slender, agile bodies.

Diet Adults feed on insects and other small invertebrates. Tadpoles eat decaying plant matter.

Reproduction When red-eyed tree frogs mate, the males come down from the canopy of the rainforest to the low-growing foliage at the edge of temporary or permanent water bodies such as pools or streams and, in a chorus of raucous croaking, call the females out of the treetops. After mating, the female lays a clutch of eggs on the underside of a leaf which is then folded around the eggs to form a tube. The tube is plugged at each end with jelly. The tadpoles hatch about six days later, wriggle through the jelly and drop into the water below. About two days later the

A UNIQUE SPECIES
The most distinctive features of
the red-eyed tree frog are its vivid
red eyes with vertical pupils. In color,
too, this tree frog is distinctive, with its
barred flanks and bluish tinges on
the limbs. Fingers and toes with
expanded, adhesive tips enable the
frog to stick to vertical surfaces.

tadpole develops limbs and the
tiny froglet leaves the water by
crawling up a small water
plant. Two weeks later it looks
like a miniature, somewhat
paler, version of the adult tree
frog. In the drier parts of the
range, the breeding season
is shorter than in those
with a long rainy season.

Habitat The red-eyed
tree frog lives in the safety
of the dense and damp tropical
rainforests of Central America.

WHITE'S TREE FROG

Also known as the common tree frog, White's tree frog *Litoria caerulea* is one of Australia's best known frogs due to its habit of visiting houses and buildings. While its natural environment is on the branches or in the hollow limbs of trees, it can often be found in bathrooms, downpipes, watertanks, letterboxes or any other damp and shaded place where it can shelter.

CLASSIFICATION

ORDER ANURA
28 FAMILIES
C. 338 GENERA • C. 4,360 SPECIES
FAMILY HYLIDAE

Characteristics A large, rather rotund frog, White's tree frog grows to about 4 inches (10 cm) in length. It is usually bright green in color, but frogs that spend more time on the ground tend to be brown. It has large climbing pads on each toe and some webbing on its hind feet. The frog's distinctive call is loud and deep, and when thousands of frogs gather to breed, the noise can be deafening.

Diet This frog feeds on insects as well as other small invertebrates and sometimes eats small mammals such as mice and rats.

Reproduction Large clumps of 2,000–3,000 eggs are laid in still water in the wet season. The eggs sink to the bottom of the pool where they hatch into large tadpoles that take about five or six weeks to metamorphose.

Habitat White's tree frog is adapted to live in all sorts of habitats from tropical forests and coastal areas to arid inland regions. It is found in northern and eastern Australia.

GLASS FROGS

Most glass frogs live high up in trees that overhang mountain streams in the cloud forests and rainforests of tropical America. Some larger species live and breed in rocky waterfalls. Their common name comes from the transparent skin on their abdomens—the result of a scarcity of pigment—which makes their internal organs visible. In some species the heart can be seen beating.

CLASSIFICATION

ORDER ANURA

28 FAMILIES
C. 338 GENERA • C. 4,360 SPECIES
FAMILY CENTROLENIDAE

Characteristics Most species are small and delicate, and bright green. They are about three-quarters to 1 inch (2–3 cm) in length. They have a wide blunt head with small eyes set almost on top of the skull.

Diet Glass frogs eat spiders and insects such as beetles and caterpillars, as well as flying insects like moths and midges.

Reproduction Clutches of eggs are laid on leaves overhanging streams. The male remains with the eggs until the tadpoles hatch and fall into the water below. Waterfall dwellers attach their eggs to rocks.

Habitat Glass frogs inhabit moist forests in Mexico and Central and South America.

Hylinobotrachium fleischmanni *is a small tree-dwelling glass frog.*

91

POISON FROGS

These are some of the most colorful and interesting frogs. Their bright gaudy hues are a warning that their skin glands secrete poisons. The toxin of one species is so potent that it used by Colombian Indians to poison their blow-gun darts. Lively little foragers, they hop about among the leaf litter on the forest floor, rarely still for longer than a second or two.

Characteristics Most of the poison frogs are small, averaging 1 to 2 inches (3–5 cm) in length. Unlike most frogs, they are active during the day. Some species have adhesive pads on their fingers and toes, and climb shrubs and trees.

Diet Most species seem to prefer ants and similarly sized arthropods which they snap up with their tongue. Unlike most frogs, they actively hunt for their prey, moving about in short hops as they search.

Reproduction Mating takes place after an elaborate courtship. Small numbers of eggs are laid in moist places and a parent, usually the male, guards the eggs. When the tadpoles hatch they wriggle onto the parent's back and are carried to water to complete their development. In some species the female releases the tadpoles into a water-holding bromeliad plant, returning occasionally to deposit an unfertilized egg into the plant as food for the tadpoles.

Habitat Poison frogs inhabit moist, tropical forests in Central and South America. Most live on the forest floor, though some are tree dwellers, and they are often found in areas near small streams.

WARNING COLORS

The poison frogs are the masters of warning coloration. Pictured here (from left to right) are the strawberry poison frog *Dendrobates pumilio*, the orange and black poison frog *Dendrobates leucomelas* and the funereal poison frog *Phyllobates lugubris*.

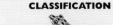

CLASSIFICATION

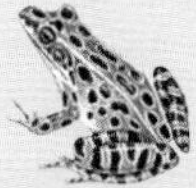

ORDER ANURA

28 FAMILIES

C. 338 GENERA • C. 4,360 SPECIES

FAMILY DENDROBATIDAE

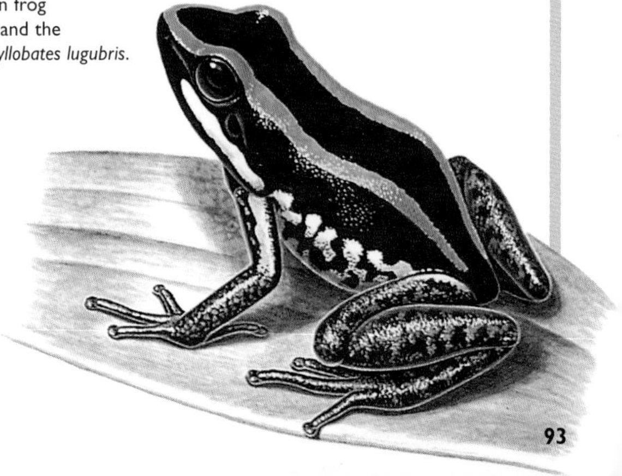

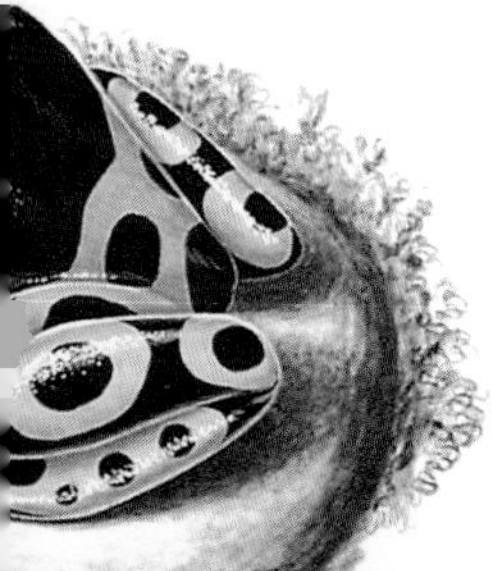

WOOD FROG

The wood frog *Rana sylvatica* is the most terrestrial of the North American frogs. Its brown and gray coloring is such a good match with its surroundings on the forest floor that when it is still it is almost invisible. The frog has very long legs and is a powerful jumper. It can leap enormous distances and never jumps twice in the same direction, thus confusing its enemies and making it harder to catch.

CLASSIFICATION

ORDER ANURA
28 FAMILIES
C. 338 GENERA • C. 4,360 SPECIES
FAMILY RANIDAE

Characteristics About 2 to 3 inches (5–7 cm) in length, the wood frog has extremely long legs that are twice the length of its head and body. It has partially webbed feet and a flat, slender body with a broad pointed head. Its coloring can be various shades of brown, from a pinkish color through to dark brown, and it has a distinct dark mask over the side of its face.

Diet The wood frog eats insects, earthworms and other small invertebrates.

Reproduction The wood frog emerges from hibernation to breed in the early spring. A globular mass of 1,000–3,000 eggs is attached to submerged vegetation in a shallow pool. If the water later freezes, the eggs do not die but continue developing as soon as higher temperatures return.

Habitat The wood frog is found in damp woods in northern North America and its range extends north of the Arctic Circle. It can survive temperatures as low as 21°F (-6°C).

SOLOMON ISLANDS TREE FROG

The Solomon Islands tree frog *Platymantis guppyi* is one of several species in the genus, all of which have limited distributions within Asia and the South Pacific. All the frogs of this genus live on islands, ranging from the southern Philippines to New Guinea and eastward through the Solomon Islands and Fiji.

CLASSIFICATION

ORDER ANURA
28 FAMILIES
C. 338 GENERA • *C.* 4,360 SPECIES
FAMILY RANIDAE

Characteristics This tree frog is well adapted to its arboreal life. It has well-developed suction pads that enable it to attach itself to tree ferns and other rainforest plants. The fingers and toes are only partly webbed.

Diet Little is known about the feeding habits of the Solomon Islands tree frog.

Reproduction This frog lays very few, large eggs with a big yolk sac. Larval development occurs inside the egg, and the young hatch as froglets without an intermediary aquatic larval stage.

Habitat This frog prefers the humid tropical forests of its island habitat. Because oceanic islands typically do not have native frogs, it is assumed that its ancestors either rafted between islands on floating vegetation or used ancient land connections.

PICKEREL FROG

The pickerel frog *Rana palustris* lives in and around brooks and streams, spending more time out of the water than in it. It retreats to the water to breed, to avoid predators such as snakes and birds, and to cool off. The bulk of its time is spent hunting for insects to eat. The frog produces an irritating secretion on its skin which has a very unpleasant odor.

CLASSIFICATION

ORDER ANURA

28 FAMILIES
C. 338 GENERA • C. 4,360 SPECIES
FAMILY RANIDAE

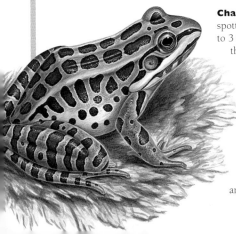

Characteristics This brown spotted, smooth-skinned frog is 2 to 3 inches (5–7 cm) in length, with the male being smaller than the female. It is an agile, powerful jumper, with long legs and webbing on its feet. It has an orange-yellow belly that "flashes" when it jumps.

Diet Pickerel frogs eat insects such as flies, beetles, butterflies, caddis flies, gnats and caterpillars as well as snails and small crustaceans.

Reproduction An irregular mass about 2 inches (5 cm) in diameter and containing 2,000–3,000 eggs is laid in shallow water in spring. The eggs hatch within a few days. The tadpoles metamorphose at different rates, some taking two, three or four months, others waiting till the following spring to turn into frogs.

Habitat Pickerel frogs live on the margins of brooks, marshes, streams and cold springs in eastern North America, as far north as Hudson Bay in Canada.

ORNATE BURROWING FROG

The ornate burrowing frog *Hildebrandtia ornata* is an African species within the wide-ranging family Ranidae—the "true" frogs. This toad-like frog usually emerges from its burrow only after rain. Like the sand frogs, the ornate burrowing frog has a squat body, short limbs and a large digging spur on the heel. It grows to just over 2 inches (5.5 cm).

CLASSIFICATION

ORDER ANURA
28 FAMILIES
C. 338 GENERA • C. 4,360 SPECIES
FAMILY RANIDAE

Characteristics This mottled brown frog can sometimes be distinguished by the green stripe along its body. Its throat is dark with a pair of distinctive white Y-shaped markings. Its pupils are horizontal. Although the fingers lack webbing, the toes are webbed.

Diet Little is known about the specific food preferences of this elusive species.

Reproduction The small eggs are laid individually in shallow water.

The tadpoles have heavy jaws and fat bodies. They grow to quite a large size before metamorphosing into adult frogs.

Habitat This frog inhabits open bushland and savanna in tropical and subtropical southern Africa.

FROG CALLS

Frogs croaking at dusk is a common sound in many parts of the world. In some tropical areas thousands of frogs may call at once, creating a chorus that can be heard more than a mile away. Frog calls vary from faint underwater chirpings to sounds that resemble an electric buzzer or the low moan of a cow.

A Mexican tree frog calling.

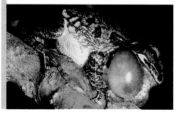

Why frogs call Female frogs are for the most part mute. It is the males that sing. A frog calls to attract a female ready to mate and to repel other males from its territory. In some species, one sort of call serves both purposes; other species may add extra notes for the territorial call or change the "tune" entirely. Each frog species has a unique call to which only members of that species will react.

How it's done Frogs were the first animals to develop a true voice. The frog forces air from its lungs through the larynx, causing the vocal chords to vibrate and produce sound. The sound is amplified and given its characteristic timber by the vocal sac or sacs. These are pouches of skin beneath the floor of the mouth or at the corner of the mouth with openings into the mouth cavity.

When calling, a frog keeps its nostrils and mouth closed and uses muscles of the body wall and throat to shunt air back and forth between the vocal sac and the lungs across the vocal chords.

More than a croak Calls range from simple, brief clicks to long, drawn-out trills of several minutes, depending on the pattern of the air flow. Different calls have been described as plonks, honks and unks, whistles, warbles and chuckles, as well as bleats, barks and duck-like quacks, to list but a few in the huge repertoire of the frog chorus. The frequency level of the call is largely determined by the frog's size, with small frogs having high-pitched calls and large frogs having low-pitched calls, but this pattern can be varied somewhat according to species.

STEALING ANOTHER GUY'S THUNDER

In some frogs and toads, like the natterjack toad, smaller males that cannot produce the louder, more rapidly repeated calls that females prefer position themselves near a large male and attempt to intercept a female attracted by the call of the larger toad.

Distinguishing species Listening to a chorus of several species calling together, a person has no difficulty in distinguishing the different calls. The frogs, however, may hear much less of the sound around them because their ears tend to be tuned to the frequency of their own species' call. Scientists as well as the frogs themselves make use of calls for distinguishing species. There are many instances where physical differences between species are very slight but where the call provides sure identification of the males, at least.

The fright scream Many frogs scream loudly when they are approached or seized. It is likely that this "distress call" or "fright scream," as it is called, is used to intimidate or startle a predator, thus giving the frog a chance to escape. The fright scream differs from other calls because it is uttered with the mouth open.

RHACOPHORID TREE FROGS

The rhacophorids, most of which are tree frogs, are relatives of the largely aquatic and terrestrial ranids or "true" frogs. There are approximately 300 species of frogs in the family, divided into 12 genera. The flying frog *Rhacophorus nigromaculatus* of Southeast Asia is a member of this family, as is the Wallace's tree frog discussed on the following page.

CLASSIFICATION

ORDER ANURA

28 FAMILIES
C. 338 GENERA • C. 4,360 SPECIES
FAMILY RHACOPHORIDAE

Characteristics Species of rhacophorid tree frogs range in size from less than 1 inch (3 cm) to 5 inches (12 cm)

Diet Depending on the species, a range of invertebrate prey is eaten.

Reproduction Most rhacophorid frogs lay their eggs in foam "nests."

TREE DWELLER
The dark-eared tree frog *Polypedates macrotis* is well adapted to its arboreal life. Its well-developed toe pads provide good adhesion.

As the eggs are produced the mating frogs use their feet to beat the eggs and seminal fluid into a froth which hardens to protect the developing eggs. Several pairs of frogs may work together to build a communal nest. The larvae remain in the nest for some time before dropping into the water to complete their development.

Habitat Rhacophorids inhabit temperate and tropical parts of Africa and Asia, including Madagascar and Japan.

WALLACE'S FLYING FROG

Wallace's flying frog *Rhacophorus nigropalmatus* lives in the upper layers of tropical rainforests. It has huge fully webbed hands and feet, with fringes of skin along its limbs that enable it to glide from tree to tree. This is usually done to escape from predators as the frog rarely launches itself unless it feels threatened. The frog grows to 4 inches (10 cm).

CLASSIFICATION

ORDER ANURA
28 FAMILIES
C. 338 GENERA • C. 4,360 SPECIES
FAMILY RHACOPHORIDAE

Characteristics This tree frog has a rather flattened body, with well-developed toe disks and loose skin on its belly to help it adhere more securely to the leaves and branches of its rainforest habitat. Its upper skin is smooth or finely granulated; the underside is coarser. Wallace's flying frog is green above, with minute white markings and one or two white patches on the thigh. Its underside is yellowish white.

Diet Like other tree frogs, this species feeds on small invertebrates.

Reproduction Like many other rhacophorids, this frog lays its eggs in a foam "nest" in a tree.

Habitat Wallace's flying frog has quite a restricted distribution. It can be found on trees and bushes in the canopies of tropical rainforests of Malaysia and Borneo.

REED AND LILY FROGS

During the day these small frogs rest on reeds and sedges at the edge of water, often motionless for hours at a time. At dusk they set up a shrill chorus and begin to look for food. They are often boldly colored and patterned, and there can be considerable variation in the markings within the same species. Some species, like the arum frog, are almost the same color as the lilies they inhabit. When it hides in the calyx of the arum lily, eating insects attracted by the nectar, this tiny, ivory-colored frog is almost invisible.

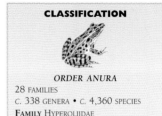

CLASSIFICATION

ORDER ANURA
28 FAMILIES
C. 338 GENERA • C. 4,360 SPECIES
FAMILY HYPEROLIIDAE

Characteristics These frogs are small, about 1 inch (2 cm) long. Most are smooth-skinned but the two species of spiny reed frogs have minute spines on their head and back which can only be seen with a magnifying glass.

Like all reed frogs, the painted reed frog Hyperolius marmoratus has expanded toe-pads and is a good climber.

Diet Reed frogs feed on flying insects such as damsel flies, mosquitoes and mites.

Reproduction Some deposit their egg masses on floating vegetation, others on plants or rocks under the water. Some lay them on leaves overhanging water. When the tadpoles hatch they drop into the water below.

Habitat Reed frogs live on the edges of lakes, ponds and swamps in Africa and Madagascar.

RUNNING FROGS

These ground-dwelling frogs prefer to walk or run rather than hop. They have bold, dark stripes that provide camouflage among the grasses in which they live. The underside is white, and ranges from smooth to slightly granular. The pupils are vertical, and the fingers lack webbing, although the toes are slightly webbed. The males issue a loud, clear "quoip" sound, with long intervals between calls.

CLASSIFICATION

ORDER ANURA

28 FAMILIES
C. 338 GENERA • C. 4,360 SPECIES
FAMILY HYPEROLIIDAE

Characteristics These are slow-moving, medium-sized frogs. The body is elongated and the limbs slender, with long digits. Their cryptic color provides good camouflage in their savanna environment.

Diet Running frogs are generally insect eaters.

Reproduction These frogs lay small pigmented eggs which they attach to submerged vegetation. Each egg is surrounded by a jelly capsule, but eggs may adhere together in small clusters.

Habitat Running frogs live in open grassland areas from the sea-shore almost to the snowline. Three species are widely distributed in southern Africa.

The Senegal running frog Kassina senegalensis *walks or runs rather than hops.*

EASTERN NARROW-MOUTHED TOAD

The eastern narrow-mouthed toad *Gastrophryne carolinensis* is completely nocturnal, spending the day in a burrow or under a log or stone. An excellent burrower, it can disappear into leaf litter or loose soil very quickly. It is rarely seen except in the breeding season when it can be found floating in pools with only the tip of its pointed head visible. At the first sign of danger it disappears beneath the surface of the water.

CLASSIFICATION

ORDER ANURA

28 FAMILIES
c. 338 GENERA • c. 4,360 SPECIES
FAMILY MICROHYLIDAE

Characteristics A stout, short-legged frog, the eastern narrow-mouthed toad grows to around 1–1½ inches (3–4 cm) in length. It has a small pointed head with tiny beady eyes and a narrow, slit-like mouth. It is a smooth-skinned, brown-patterned frog with a loose fold of skin extending across the head behind the eyes. There is a spade for digging on each hind foot. It has a croak which sounds like the weak bleat of a sheep.

Diet The toad eats a variety of insects but it prefers ants.

Reproduction The frogs usually mate after rain. Small eggs are laid in stagnant water where they float on the surface in a thin sheet.

Habitat The frog lives near bodies of still water, especially along the edges of ponds and ditches, and under moist decaying plant and leaf litter. It is found mainly in south-eastern USA with a few populations in northern USA.

RED-BANDED CREVICE CREEPER

Because its smooth skin is rubbery in texture, the red-banded crevice creeper *Phrynomerus bifasciatus* is sometimes known as the rubber frog, or the rubber banded frog. It is a nocturnal rock dweller which during dry seasons takes refuge in tree hollows and burrows. Its bright colors warn potential predators of the dangers of its toxic skin. Lighting conditions can bring about significant changes in skin color.

CLASSIFICATION

ORDER ANURA

28 FAMILIES
C. 338 GENERA • C. 4,360 SPECIES
FAMILY MICROHYLIDAE

Characteristics This pear-shaped, frog reaches lengths of around 3 inches (7 cm). Its sound is a loud melodious trill sustained over one or two seconds. The pupil is circular. The fingers lack webbing, and there is scanty webbing on the toes.

Diet This is an insect-eating frog, with ants forming an important part of its diet.

Reproduction The frog breeds in floodwaters or other shallow waters, where the eggs are laid in a large mass on the surface.

Habitat The red-banded crevice creeper is an African species, distributed south of the Sahara.

PARADOX FROG

The paradox frog *Pseudis paradoxa* is famous for its gigantic tadpoles which can grow up to four times the length of the adults. It is an excellent swimmer and lives in shallow lakes, ponds and swamps where there is plenty of plant life. The frog floats among the vegetation, searching for food by stirring up the mud with its fingers and toes. The paradox frog survives very dry periods by burying itself in mud.

CLASSIFICATION

ORDER ANURA

28 FAMILIES
C. 338 GENERA • C. 4,360 SPECIES
FAMILY PSEUDIDAE

Characteristics The paradox frog has extremely powerful hindlimbs, huge fully webbed feet with long slender fingers and toes, and is about 3 inches (7 cm) in length. It has extraordinarily slippery skin and cryptic coloring which help it to elude predators such as snakes and fish.

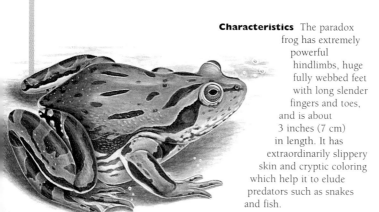

Diet These frogs eat small aquatic invertebrates.

Reproduction The eggs are laid in a frothy mass on the surface of the water. The tadpoles reach lengths of up to 10 inches (25 cm) before metamorphosing into the more moderate-sized adults. The tadpoles reach their full size in four months.

Habitat The paradox frog lives in still, richly vegetated bodies of water in the tropical lowlands of northern South America.

GHOST FROGS

These frogs have rather flat bodies and well-developed adhesive pads on their fingers and toes. They are therefore well adapted to fit into crevices and to cling to slippery rocks along the cool, shaded mountain streams where they live. Their common name may have been coined because one species is found in a place called Skeleton Gorge; certainly there is little else ghostly about them.

CLASSIFICATION

ORDER ANURA
28 FAMILIES
C. 338 GENERA • C. 4,360 SPECIES
FAMILY HELEOPHRYNIDAE

Characteristics These are small to medium-sized frogs, about $2^{1}/_{2}$ inches (6.5 cm) in length. They have long legs and heavily webbed feet for swimming. Their underside is covered with thin white skin, so thin that their digestive organs can be seen through it. They have a flat head and very prominent eyes.

Diet These frogs are very rarely encountered, but it is generally assumed that their main diet is insects.

Reproduction The eggs are large and are laid beneath wet stones in shallow backwaters. The tadpoles have sucker-like mouths which enable them to cling to rocks while feeding in swiftly flowing water.

Habitat The frogs live in and around fast-flowing mountain streams in the Cape and Transvaal regions of South Africa.

The Cape ghost frog Heleophryne purcelli has been seen leaping up at flies and capturing them to eat.

NEW ZEALAND FROGS

There are only three frog species native to New Zealand. They are small, secretive, nocturnal animals that shelter by day under stones and logs or in damp crevices. Archey's frog and Hamilton's frog lay their eggs on land. When the tadpoles hatch, they climb onto the male's back where they stay until they metamorphose. The tadpoles of the semi-aquatic Hochstetter's frog develop in water.

CLASSIFICATION

ORDER ANURA
28 FAMILIES • C. 338 GENERA •
C. 4,360 SPECIES
FAMILY LEIOPELMATIDAE

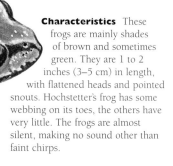

Characteristics These frogs are mainly shades of brown and sometimes green. They are 1 to 2 inches (3–5 cm) in length, with flattened heads and pointed snouts. Hochstetter's frog has some webbing on its toes, the others have very little. The frogs are almost silent, making no sound other than faint chirps.

Three frogs are endemic to New Zealand. All are small, nocturnal egg-laying species.

Diet Insects and spiders are the main part of the frogs' diet, but they will eat any prey that they can catch.

Reproduction These frogs lay their four to 19 large, yolky eggs in moist soil under rocks and logs.

Habitat The frogs inhabit damp, forested areas. Hochstetter's frog, the most widespread, lives on the edges of shady creeks and is found on the North Island. Archey's frog is restricted to a small area of the North Island and Hamilton's frog to two small islands.

SEYCHELLES FROGS

On the Seychelles Islands there are three species of small, terrestrial frogs. Unlike most other frogs, they lay their eggs on the ground rather than in water. The female of one species, *Sooglossus sechellensis*, guards her eggs and when they hatch, the tadpoles climb onto her back where she carries them until a short time after they have metamorphosed into small froglets.

CLASSIFICATION

ORDER ANURA
28 FAMILIES • C. 338 GENERA •
C. 4,360 SPECIES
FAMILY SOOGLOSSIDAE

Characteristics The Seychelles frogs grow to about 1½ inches (4 cm) in length. At less than half an inch (1 cm) long, *Sooglussus gardineri* is one of the world's smallest frogs. They are green or brown in color, with long legs and a slender body. *Nesomantis thomasseti* is more toad-like than the other two species.

Diet These frogs feed on small invertebrates.

Reproduction The eggs are laid in small clumps on moist ground.

Those of *S. gardineri* complete their development to adult frogs on the ground. However, scientists do not know what happens to the eggs of *N. thomasseti*.

Habitat These frogs live in rotting plant matter on the floor of moss forests, and are found only on the Seychelles Islands.

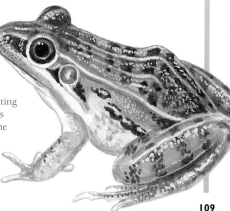

The frogs of the Sooglossus genus are tiny terrestrial species endemic to the Sychelles Islands.

109

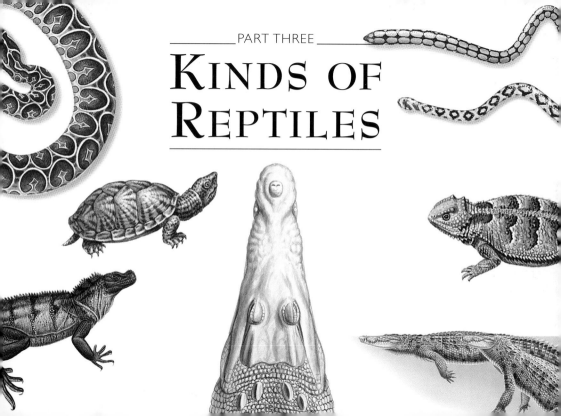

PART THREE

KINDS OF
REPTILES

TURTLES AND TORTOISES

Turtles and tortoises are the oldest reptile forms on Earth and they have changed very little in the 230 million years since they first appeared. Turtles and tortoises are the only reptiles that have a shell built into their skeleton and they are divided into two suborders according to the way they draw their heads into this shell. There are about 200 species of hidden-necked, or straight-necked, turtles which have flexible necks that they can pull straight back into their shells. The 70 or so species of side-necked turtles bend their neck sideways and tuck their heads in under the front edge of the upper shell.

SIDE-NECKED TURTLES

The side-necked turtles in the family Chelidae are well adapted to life in fresh water. The long neck of most species allows them to draw breath at the surface of the water without exposing the rest of the body to potential predators, and they can stay underwater for lengthy periods while searching for food. In seasonally dry areas, some species will burrow deep into the mud at the bottom of lagoons and swamps where they remain dormant till the rain comes again.

CRYPTIC COLORS
The South American twist-necked turtle
Platemys platycephala is a poor swimmer
that walks along the bottom of streams. Its
disruptive coloration camouflages it on
the leaf-strewn forest floor or stream bed.

Characteristics These turtles vary in size from the endangered western swamp turtle of Western Australia which has a shell length of 5½ inches (14 cm) to the South American spotted-bellied side-necked turtle which reaches lengths of 17 inches (44 cm). Some species, the short-necked turtles and snapping turtles, have shorter necks and are excellent swimmers.

Diet The side-necked turtles prefer to feed on insects, crayfish, tadpoles, and also small fish and frogs. Some species eat water plants as well as the fruit that falls into the water from surrounding trees.

Reproduction Clutches of one to 25 eggs are laid in soil or in sandy river banks. The Australian northern snake-necked turtle is the only turtle to lay its eggs underwater.

Habitat These turtles are aquatic and semi-aquatic. Some species live in still water like swamps, lakes and pools. Others prefer the running water of rivers. They are found in Australia, New Guinea and South America.

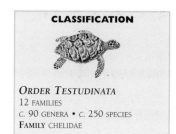

CLASSIFICATION

ORDER TESTUDINATA
12 FAMILIES
C. 90 GENERA • C. 250 SPECIES
FAMILY CHELIDAE

The Sepik turtle Elseya novaeguineae is a short-necked turtle which inhabits streams and lakes in New Guinea.

HELMETED SIDE-NECKED TURTLES

This family of side-necked turtles occurs only in South America, Africa and Madagascar. Giant side-necked river turtles are a common sight on the sand banks of the Amazon and Orinoco rivers when they are nesting. The African species live in both flowing and still water but prefer to hide in the mud where they find their food and where they bury themselves in the dry season to aestivate.

CLASSIFICATION

ORDER TESTUDINATA
12 FAMILIES
C. 90 GENERA • C. 250 SPECIES
FAMILY PELOMEDUSIDAE

The yellow-spotted Amazon River turtle
Podocnemis unifilis *is mainly a plant eater but sometimes filters particles from the water's surface.*

Characteristics The turtles range in size from the 5-inch (12-cm) African dwarf mud turtle to the 3-foot (1-m) South American river turtle. The African species have strong-smelling musk glands which deter predators.

Diet Some species eat mollusks, worms and insects. Others, such as the South America river turtles, are predominantly plant eaters.

Reproduction Depending on the size of the turtle, clutches of four to more than 150 eggs are laid in a chamber excavated in soil or in a sandy riverbank.

Habitat These freshwater turtles are aquatic and semi-aquatic. Some live in and around flowing rivers and streams. Others prefer the still water of ponds and swamps, and even temporary floodwaters. They are found in tropical South America, Africa south of the Sahara and Madagascar.

Big-headed Turtle

This unique Asian turtle cannot retract its huge head nor its long, heavily armored tail into its shell. It's a poor swimmer, preferring to walk along the bed of the mountain streams where it lives, but it can climb well. It is well adapted to grasp and move among the large boulders on the stream bottom and is sometimes seen basking on the lower branches of bushes and trees at the edge of the water.

CLASSIFICATION

ORDER TESTUDINATA
12 FAMILIES
C. 90 GENERA • C. 250 SPECIES
FAMILY CHELYDRIDAE

Characteristics The turtle is rarely more than 8 inches (20 cm) in shell length. Its flattened shell is too small to enclose the fleshy parts of its body. Both the head and tail are covered with large horny scales, and it has very strong, beak-like jaws which it uses to grasp its prey tightly and to bite through their thick shells.

Diet The turtle emerges at night to hunt snails, crabs and mollusks.

Reproduction The reproductive rate of this turtle is low with only one or two eggs being laid in a nest dug by the female in the bank of a stream. In its natural environment, this low rate is not a problem as the turtle has few predators.

Habitat The big-headed turtle lives in cool, fast-flowing mountain streams. It is found in southern China, and northern and central Indo-China.

Platysternon megacephalum shiui, *a big-headed turtle from Vietnam.*

117

A TURTLE'S SHELL

All turtles and tortoises have a shell which is built into their skeleton. Many can pull their heads and legs inside the shell, thus giving them protection from predators. The shell also prevents moisture loss when water is scarce and absorbs heat to keep the turtle warm.

scute

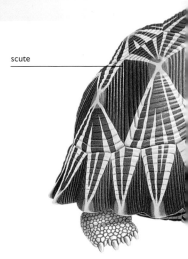

Shell parts A turtle's shell has two main parts: the upper shell, or carapace; and the lower shell, or plastron. The shell is constructed of interconnected bony plates. The ribs and backbone are fused to the carapace. Both the carapace and the plastron are covered by a second outer layer of large horny plates, or scutes. Only the softshell turtles, the Papuan softshell turtle and the leatherback turtle do not have these horny plates on the shell.

Shell shape Shells vary in color, hardness and shape. The shape of turtles' shells often points to how they move and the environment they live in.

Slow-moving land tortoises have thick, dome-shaped shells for protection.

Semi-terrestrial turtles have a semi-domed shell to suit their lives on both land and water.

Pond turtles have small, flattened, usually lighter, shells for swimming.

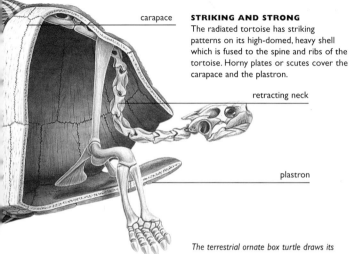

carapace

STRIKING AND STRONG

The radiated tortoise has striking patterns on its high-domed, heavy shell which is fused to the spine and ribs of the tortoise. Horny plates or scutes cover the carapace and the plastron.

retracting neck

plastron

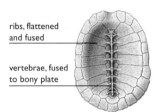

A turtle's carapace viewed from below.

ribs, flattened and fused

vertebrae, fused to bony plate

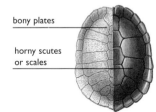

A turtle's carapace, viewed from above.

bony plates

horny scutes or scales

Sea turtles have light, streamlined shells for swimming.

The terrestrial ornate box turtle draws its head and legs into its domed shell for protection against predators and drying out.

119

SNAPPING TURTLES

The two species of snapping turtles are famous for their swift, savage bite. They lie in wait and ambush their prey, snapping it up with their powerful jaws. The American snapping turtle, the smaller of the two species, spends much of its time in water, though it does like to sunbathe in the mornings on the banks of streams and swamps. The alligator snapping turtle is even more aquatic. Large older animals rarely leave the water, and then only the females to lay eggs.

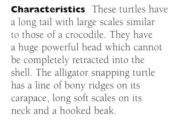

Characteristics These turtles have a long tail with large scales similar to those of a crocodile. They have a huge powerful head which cannot be completely retracted into the shell. The alligator snapping turtle has a line of bony ridges on its carapace, long soft scales on its neck and a hooked beak.

Diet The American snapping turtle is mainly carnivorous, feeding on frogs, salamanders, fish, and small birds and mammals. The alligator snapping turtle eats virtually anything it can capture—even small turtles, large snails and mussels are unable to resist its strong jaws.

Reproduction Both species dig a nest chamber, usually well away from water, and lay 20 to 40 eggs.

Habitat The American snapping turtle lives in freshwater swamps and streams from southern Canada to Ecuador. The alligator snapping

CLASSIFICATION

ORDER TESTUDINATA
12 FAMILIES
C. 90 GENERA • *C.* 250 SPECIES
FAMILY CHELYDRIDAE

turtle lives in rivers, lakes and large swamps in south-eastern USA.

An American snapping turtle Chelydra serpentina *snaps up a snake.*

NEW WORLD POND TURTLES

The best known pond turtles are the ornamented turtles—the beautiful painted turtles, sliders and cooters. They have brightly colored shells, heads and limbs. Many species like to bask in the sun, especially in the early morning when they congregate along the banks of rivers and ponds to raise their body temperature, though always prepared to plunge into deeper water if alarmed.

A male painted turtle Chrysemys picta belli *from North America.*

Characteristics Pond turtles have a bony shell covered with horny plates, and some species have well-developed hinges on the plastron that can completely close the shell. They also have well-developed limbs with webbed feet. In a number of species, the males are much smaller than the females.

Diet There is considerable variation in diet between species, even between sexes and individuals. For example, the much larger female map turtles, which live in deeper water, have a largely vegetarian diet, while the smaller males favor a more carnivorous diet in the shallows. In some species the adults are more vegetarian while the young feed mainly on insects. Species living in brackish water eat a broad range of food including crustaceans, mollusks and aquatic plants.

Reproduction Most New World pond turtles dig a nest or cavity in

A painted turtle Chrysemys picta picta *basks on a log.*

CLASSIFICATION

ORDER TESTUDINATA
12 FAMILIES
C. 90 GENERA • C. 250 SPECIES
FAMILY EMYDIDAE

which five to 10 eggs are laid. Often several clutches are laid in a season.

Habitat Most pond turtles are semi-aquatic and live in swamps, pools, ditches, rivers, and even coastal lagoons and estuaries. Some, like the box turtles, are more terrestrial and live in grasslands, prairies and woodlands far from water. New World pond turtles occur in the Caribbean, and North, Central and South America, with one species, the European pond turtle, in Europe, North Africa and the Middle East.

The eastern box turtle Terrapene carolina carolina *can withdraw its head, limbs and tail into its shell.*

123

OLD WORLD POND TURTLES

There are many similarities between these and the New World pond turtles. Many are mostly aquatic, leaving the water only to sunbathe or lay eggs. Others are decidedly amphibious. The Mediterranean turtle and Caspian turtle, for example, live in arid and mountainous areas where the streams tend to dry up in the summer. They migrate overland, often long distances, to find new sources of water. If they find none, they bury themselves until it rains.

The Malayan snail-eating turtle Malayemys subtrijuga lives in still or slow waters.

Characteristics River turtles, the largest of all the pond turtles, have a distinctive solid shell and strong, fully webbed feet. The biggest, the Malaysian giant turtle, has a shell length of 31 inches (80 cm). The smallest pond turtle, the bog turtle, measures 11 inches (28 cm). The amphibious hinged tortoises of Asia have a plastral hinge that allows the turtle to withdraw its head and limbs into a completely closed shell. Some terrestrial species have colors and markings that provide them with camouflage on the forest floor. The warm yellow, orange and brown patterns of the Indochinese box turtle make it almost invisible amongst the leaf litter. The shells of the keeled box turtle and the black-breasted leaf turtle have serrated edges that, along with their variegated brown color, give the turtles a leaf-like appearance when they are still.

Diet Young river turtles tend to be omnivorous but are strictly vegetarian when adult. Most other aquatic species are also vegetarian, one exception being the Malayan snail-eating turtle which feeds primarily on mollusks. The amphibious and terrestrial species tend to be omnivorous, though the land turtles are predominantly herbivores.

Reproduction Small species lay one or two eggs, larger species around thirty. The painted terrapin of Asia often lays its eggs on beaches. The young live briefly in the sea then make their way to estuaries and rivers.

Habitat Aquatic species live in estuaries, rivers and lakes; semi-aquatic species in forested ponds, streams and marshes; and terrestrial species in woodlands and mountain forests. They are found in Europe, North Africa, Asia and Central and South America.

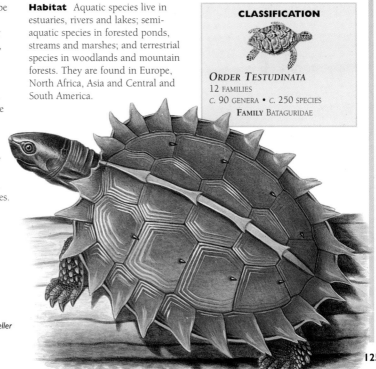

CLASSIFICATION

ORDER TESTUDINATA
12 FAMILIES
C. 90 GENERA • C. 250 SPECIES
FAMILY BATAGURIDAE

The spined or cogwheel turtle **Heosemys spinosa** *is a forest dweller from South-East Asia.*

LAND TORTOISES

Land tortoises from temperate regions are dependent on seasonal supplies of fresh herby plants and spend the colder months hibernating underground. In hot dry regions, land tortoises are active only in the morning and late afternoon. During the heat of the day they rest in the shade of shrubs and trees or in burrows in the earth. Some take refuge in underground burrows during the dry parts of the year.

Characteristics Most land tortoises have high-domed, heavy shells that make them slow-moving. When threatened, many can retract their heads and all or most of their limbs into the shell. They have strong stumpy legs with claws.

Diet All land tortoises are mainly vegetarian, though they will eat insects, worms, crustaceans, mollusks, and even carrion and the dung of hoofed animals.

The radiated tortoise Asterochelys radiata is an endangered species from Madagascar.

The African pancake tortoise Malacochersus tornieri has a flat, flexible shell that allows it to squeeze into crevices in its rocky habitat.

ALL SIZES
Land tortoises range in length from the 4-in (10-cm) Madagascan spider tortoises to the 51-in (130-cm) wheelbarrow-sized giants of the Aldabra Islands.

CLASSIFICATION

ORDER TESTUDINATA
12 FAMILIES
C. 90 GENERA • C. 250 SPECIES
FAMILY TESTUDINAE

Reproduction The eggs of all land tortoises have a calcified shell that is resistant to damage and drying out. To make digging a nest easier in often hard ground, the females may release urine and water (stored in their anal sac) to soften the soil.

Habitat Land tortoises are found in Europe, Africa, Asia and all the Americas as well as on islands such as the Seychelles, Aldabra and the Galapagos. They live in various habitats, from deserts to rainforests.

GALAPAGOS GIANTS

The Galapagos Islands in the Pacific Ocean are home to populations of giant tortoises that were isolated from each other many thousands of years ago. The groups on the different islands adapted differently. Tortoises on the large, wetter islands have developed big dome-like shells, and consequently are known as "domes." Tortoises on the smaller, drier islands where plants grow tall have long legs and a smaller "saddleback" shell which is raised in front so the tortoises can stretch their necks to reach up to the plants.

SADDLEBACK STRETCH

In dry times, the giant saddleback tortoises get water and food from tall cactus plants which are very fleshy and contain lots of moisture. When it does rain, dozens of tortoises collect around the puddles and drink as much as they can.

A saddleback Galapagos giant turtle Chelonoidis elephantopus.

Characteristics Like other giant species, the bones in the shells of the Galapagos tortoises have a honeycomb structure which encloses many small air chambers. If the bony shell were solid, it would be difficult for the tortoise to carry it around. They weigh 330–440 pounds (150–200 kg) with lengths up to 43 inches (110 cm) and have elephantine limbs and feet.

Diet The giant tortoise's diet includes grass and other herbaceous plants and leaves from bushes.

Reproduction Mating occurs after a fairly intimidating courtship where the male rams the female with his shell and nips at her legs until she is forced to draw them in, thus immobilizing her. The female lays clutches of around 10 eggs in a nest in the completely dry lava soils of the lowlands of the islands. The time of incubation varies from three to eight months, depending on the temperature. Most baby tortoises die in the first 10 years of life.

Habitat The tortoises live on seven islands in the center of the Galapagos archipelago. In the cooler months they live on the grassy lowlands. During the hot, dry season they travel up to the volcanic highlands to wallow in the water, to feed on the plantlife there, and to shelter in the shade.

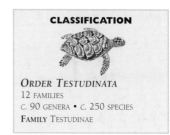

CLASSIFICATION

ORDER TESTUDINATA
12 FAMILIES
C. 90 GENERA • C. 250 SPECIES
FAMILY TESTUDINAE

Like all turtles, the Galapagos giants have no teeth. They use their sharp-edged jaws to grasp and cut plant food.

129

SOFTSHELL TURTLES

Instead of an outer horny layer on their carapace, the softshell turtles have a leathery skin. This lighter, more flexible shell suits their aquatic existence. They are fast swimmers in open water and can stay underwater longer than most aquatic turtles. They are able to take in oxygen from the water through the lining of their throat and also through their skin. They lie hidden from predators on the muddy beds of streams and lakes.

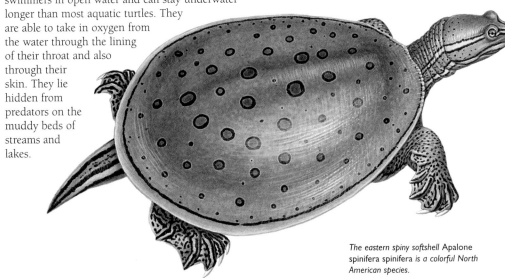

The eastern spiny softshell Apalone spinifera spinifera *is a colorful North American species.*

Characteristics Softshell turtles have knife-sharp horny jaws which they can use to defend themselves. Despite their many adaptations to aquatic life, those in northern latitudes regularly come onto land to sunbathe. The smallest softshell is the 12-inch (30-cm) Indian flapshell turtle, one of several species that have large flaps of skin on the plastron to cover the hind feet. The largest is the Asian giant softshell turtle with a shell length of 51 inches (130 cm).

Diet Most softshell turtles are strictly carnivorous, feeding on mollusks, crustaceans, aquatic insects, worms, frogs and fish. A few species also eat fruit and aquatic plants.

Reproduction Most softshell turtles lay about 10 to 20 eggs. They are about an inch (3 cm) in diameter and are laid in a nest excavated on a beach or in a river bank or a river sandbar.

Habitat These turtles live in freshwater rivers, lakes and streams, with some inhabiting the brackish estuaries of larger rivers. They are found in North America, Africa and Asia.

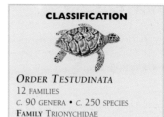

CLASSIFICATION

ORDER TESTUDINATA
12 FAMILIES
C. 90 GENERA • C. 250 SPECIES
FAMILY TRIONYCHIDAE

ADAPTED FOR WATER
With their smooth flat shell, large webbed feet, and a snorkel-shaped snout that allows them to breathe while keeping the rest of their body under the surface, the softshell turtles are custom-built for life in the water.

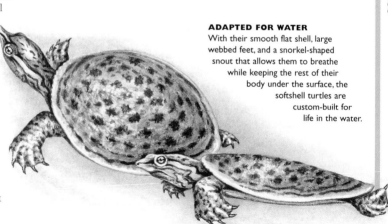

MUD TURTLES

Most of these are inconspicuous, brown colored turtles which spend the greater part of their day walking on the bottom of streams and lakes looking for food. In the mornings they leave the water to bask in the sun to achieve their preferred body temperature. Many species, especially the smaller ones, climb shrubs and even trees at the water's edge.

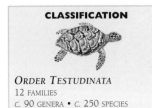

CLASSIFICATION

ORDER TESTUDINATA
12 FAMILIES
C. 90 GENERA • C. 250 SPECIES
FAMILY KINOSTERNIDAE

The yellow mud turtle Kinosternon flavescens *is found in Mexico and the USA.*

Characteristics The average size of these turtles is 6–8 inches (15–20 cm). All species have a solid carapace which is covered by strong, occasionally overlapping, horny shields. The plastron is hinged at the front and the back so the turtle can completely close the shell.

Diet All mud turtles are carnivorous. They eat worms, insects, mollusks, crustaceans, fish and amphibians.

Reproduction Several clutches of one to six eggs are laid each year. Some species lay them under leaf litter or in rotting logs, others excavate a shallow nest chamber.

Habitat The semi-aquatic mud turtles are found in and around the edges of lakes, streams and ponds in the USA, Central America and northern South America.

MUSK TURTLES

The four species of musk turtles (left) found in the United States are often called "stinkpot" turtles because of the extraordinarily strong musky smell they release when they are captured or disturbed. Musk turtles from Central America also produce this odor and they have sharp horny beaks as well which they use to defend themselves effectively. Musk turtles are closely related to the mud turtles and have a similar lifestyle.

CLASSIFICATION

ORDER TESTUDINATA
12 FAMILIES
C. 90 GENERA • C. 250 SPECIES
FAMILY KINOSTERNIDAE

Characteristics Most musk turtles have a reduced plastron. In the cross-breasted turtles of Central America it is a strong, bony cross. The turtles are small, with an average shell length of 6–8 inches (15–20 cm).

Diet The turtles are omnivorous. They eat insects, spiders, mollusks, fish, amphibians and aquatic plants.

Reproduction Most species lay several clutches of two to five eggs each season. The eggs are laid under fallen timber or in dense leaf litter, or in a shallow, excavated nest chamber.

Habitat Musk turtles are semi-aquatic and live in lakes, streams and ponds in central and southern USA and in Central America.

The southern loggerhead musk turtle Sternotherus minor minor is a small freshwater turtle of southern North America.

REPRODUCTION AND THE YOUNG

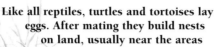

Like all reptiles, turtles and tortoises lay eggs. After mating they build nests on land, usually near the areas where they live and feed, though some sea and river turtles migrate long distances to lay their eggs, thousands of miles in the case of many sea turtles.

THE NEST
Most turtles lay their eggs in a funnel- or flask-shaped chamber in sand or soil which the female digs with her hindlimbs. A few lay their eggs in burrows, in the nests of other animals, or under leaf litter or decaying plant matter.

Courtship Behavior varies from the male simply mounting the female, usually in semi-aquatic species where the male is bigger than the female, to quite elaborate displays. The male painted turtle, for example, uses the long claws on his forelimbs in a complex dance ritual. He swims in front of the female and rhythmically strokes both sides of her head with his claws until she is ready to mate. Courtship in tortoises usually involves some head-bobbing, with

RACE TO THE SEA

Guided by the low open horizon, newborn flatback turtles race to the sea, safety in numbers being the only thing that saves some of them from predatory birds and crabs. Those that reach the sea are still not safe as sharks and other fish wait for them in the shallow water.

The hatchlings Once the eggs are covered over, the parents show no interest in the young. In many species, the hatchlings spend the winter in the egg chamber, appearing for the first time in the spring. From the day they leave the nest the young must fend for themselves. Scientists estimate that only about one turtle in 100 will live to become an adult.

Olive ridley turtles mate offshore from the nesting beach.

the male head-butting and biting the female to immobilize her.

Eggs Small species generally lay a few eggs (one to six) while many of the large species lay clutches of 150 or more. The average incubation time is two to three months with some larger species taking a year or longer. The temperature of the nest can also be a factor in the speed of development. In some species, such as pond and snapping turtles, this temperature also determines the sex of the hatchlings.

135

HARDBACK SEA TURTLES

With their flattened, streamlined shells and large front flippers, sea turtles are built for life in the ocean. They can swim at speeds of up to 18 miles (29 km) per hour when escaping from predators such as sharks. Usually they swim much more slowly, using the ocean currents to help them search for food. The males never leave the water and the females do so only to lay eggs. They often sunbathe at the surface, drifting on floating fields of seaweed, or in shallow water left by the receding tide on coral reefs.

LONG DISTANCE TRAVELERS

Some green sea turtles *Chelonia mydas* migrate from the coast of Brazil to nesting beaches on Ascension Island in the mid-Atlantic Ocean, a distance of 3,000 miles (5,000 km). Probably because of the length of this journey, the turtles breed only every two or three years.

Characteristics The shells of hardback sea turtles have a complete covering of horny plates. Their forelimbs are more strongly developed than their hindlimbs, a feature distinguishing them from freshwater species, and they are shaped like paddles or flippers. The turtles use their forelimbs to move through the water, the hindlimbs serving chiefly as rudders. The shell is lighter than freshwater species as between the bony plates of the carapace and the plastron there are areas of fibrous skin. Sea turtles cannot retract their heads inside their shells. They vary in size from the ridley sea turtles which rarely have a shell length of more than 28 inches (70 cm) to the loggerhead turtle that can reach lengths of 7 feet (2 m).

Diet Most sea turtles are chiefly carnivorous. They eat fish, jellyfish, sponges, crabs, clams, mussels and sea urchins. Some species also eat marine plants and the green turtle grazes on seagrasses.

Reproduction Sea turtles travel vast distances across the oceans to breed. The two sexes rendezvous and mate at sea near the nesting beaches, often the same beach at which they themselves were hatched. The female comes ashore at night to lay the eggs. She builds a nest in the sand or dunes above the high-tide line. The clutches are large, varying from 80 to 200. Several clutches may be laid at two- or three-week intervals, though she will lay only every two or three years. Tales are told of females crying as they lay their eggs but in fact sea turtles produce these "tears" all the time from special glands close to the eyes to get rid of salt.

Habitat Sea turtles are found in all the tropical and subtropical oceans the world.

CLASSIFICATION

ORDER TESTUDINATA
12 FAMILIES
C. 90 GENERA• C. 250 SPECIES
FAMILY CHELONIIDAE

ENDANGERED TURTLES
Sea turtles have been hunted for their eggs, meat, shell and skin so many are endangered. The much sought-after "tortoise shell" of the Pacific hawksbill turtle *Eretmochelys imbricata* has put the species at great risk. The horny shields of its upper shell are beautifully marbled and are used in the manufacture of items from spectacle frames to hair brushes.

LEATHERBACK TURTLE

The largest turtle alive today is the leatherback turtle *Dermochelys coriacea*, the only survivor of an otherwise extinct family. Unlike the other sea turtles, whose shells are covered by horny plates, the shell of this species is covered by a leathery skin. It is a powerful swimmer and when its huge, paddle-like forelimbs are in motion in the open ocean, the fast-moving turtle is an impressive sight.

Characteristics One 8-foot (2.5 m) individual has been recorded but turtles with shell lengths of more than about 5 feet (1.5 m) are uncommon. The span from the tip of one front flipper to the tip of the other is greater than the length of the shell. The turtles have a large head with big eyes and a hooked beak.

Diet The leatherback turtle feeds mainly on jellyfish but also eats mollusks, crustaceans like swimmer crabs, and echinoderms like sea urchins and sea stars.

Reproduction Like all sea turtles, the females return to the same beaches over and over again to lay their eggs, usually the same beach where they themselves were hatched. They lay several clutches of 50 to 170 eggs at 10-day intervals, every two or three years.

Habitat The turtles are found in tropical and temperate seas throughout the world, and sometimes in the colder waters of higher latitudes. They lay their eggs on tropical beaches.

CLASSIFICATION

ORDER TESTUDINATA
12 FAMILIES
C. 90 GENERA • C. 250 SPECIES
FAMILY DERMOCHELYIDAE

CROCODILES AND ALLIGATORS

During the Mesozoic era 245 to 65 million years ago, the Archosauria, or "ruling reptiles," dominated the land. The only giant archosaurs to survive to modern times are the crocodilians. The order Crocodilia includes the largest and some of the most dangerous of the world's living reptiles, and they are amongst the largest of the vertebrates that still venture onto land. The order contains the crocodiles, alligators, caimans and gharials.

AMERICAN ALLIGATOR

When the American alligator *Alligator mississippiensis* spots its prey, it submerges all of its body but the top of its head and swims soundlessly through the water until it is close enough to attack. So smoothly does it glide through the murky swamp water that the vegetation on the surface is scarcely disturbed. This same silent hunter is also the noisiest of all the crocodilians. During the breeding season, a territorial male utters loud, bellowing roars that can be heard 500 feet (150 m) away. Its neighbors respond in choruses that may last half an hour or more.

JUMP SHOT

American alligators often hunt near water-bird colonies where they eat the fish that gather to feed on the birds' droppings. Occasionally an alligator will leap from the water to catch a bird such as this egret chick which has fallen from its nest.

Characteristics

The black American alligator grows to 20 feet (6 m) in length. Its snout is moderately long and wide, and it has blunt broad jaws which help it catch prey in thick vegetation.

Diet Young alligators eat insects. As they grow larger, snakes, turtles, snails, fish, small mammals and birds are added to their diet. Large adults sometimes take small calves and, very occasionally, people.

Reproduction The female scratches soil and vegetation into a pile, repeatedly dragging her body over the nest until it is compacted into a mound. She then scoops out a cavity in the center of the mound with her hind feet and lays a clutch of about 35–40 large eggs which take nine weeks to hatch.

Habitat American alligators live in swamps, ponds, rivers, lakes and estuaries in south-eastern USA.

CLASSIFICATION

ORDER CROCODILIA
3 FAMILIES • 8 GENERA • C. 23 SPECIES
FAMILY ALLIGATORIDAE

CHINESE ALLIGATOR

Like its American relative, the Chinese alligator *Alligator sinensis* can tolerate much colder temperatures than other crocodilians. In winter, alligators retreat into burrows under river banks and in mud holes. Or they move to shallow backwaters where the larger animals can survive freezing conditions by keeping their nose above the water so that breathing holes form when the surface of the water freezes. Here they remain dormant until the temperature rises.

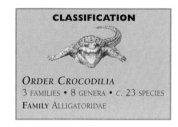

CLASSIFICATION

ORDER CROCODILIA
3 FAMILIES • 8 GENERA • C. 23 SPECIES
FAMILY ALLIGATORIDAE

Characteristics The Chinese alligator rarely exceeds 7 feet (2 m). It has a broad, heavy head and its back and neck are heavily armored with overlapping plates.

Diet Snails, clams, rats and insects form most of the alligator's diet.

Reproduction The female builds a mound nest similar to the American alligator but slightly smaller. It lays around 10–40 eggs.

Habitat The Chinese alligator lives in the muddy waters of the Yangzte River and its tributaries in China. The alligator is critically endangered because human population pressures and natural disasters such as floods threaten its habitat.

Breaking through the ice.

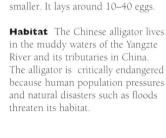

CUVIER'S DWARF CAIMAN

Along with Schneider's dwarf caiman, Cuvier's dwarf caiman *Paleosuchus palpebrosus* is the most heavily armored crocodilian; even its eyelids are protected by bony plates. These two caimans are sometimes called smooth-fronted caimans because they do not have a bony ridge between their eyes like other caimans. They seem to have a more terrestrial lifestyle than other crocodilians with adults spending much of their time away from water.

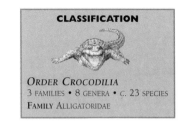

CLASSIFICATION

ORDER CROCODILIA
3 FAMILIES • 8 GENERA • C. 23 SPECIES
FAMILY ALLIGATORIDAE

Characteristics The smallest crocodilian, male Cuvier's dwarf caimans reach about 5 feet (1.5 m) in length, females about 4 feet (1.2 m). They have a skull that is high, smooth and dog-like, the only crocodilians with this head shape. Unlike most other crocodilians, which have yellowish eyes, the dwarf caimans have rich brown eyes.

Diet Cuvier's dwarf caiman eats invertebrates and fish.

Reproduction Mound nests have been found but little else is known about this species in the wild.

Habitat This caiman lives in gallery forests in savannas or in forests on the margins of large lakes and rivers. It is found in the Amazon, Orinoco and Sao Francisco river systems and also in the upper reaches of the Parana and Paraguay river systems.

COMMON CAIMAN

Widespread in South America, the common caiman *Caiman crocodilus* is probably the only crocodilian in the world that responds favorably to changes in its habitat. When people construct dams or lagoons to water cattle, or excavate earth from pits that soon become vegetated and fill with water, the caiman moves in. If its pools dry out, it will walk long distances across land to find permanent water.

ON LAND

When the common caiman moves across land in search of water and new hunting territories, it moves slowly on its short legs. It may find some carrion to eat along the way, but it is unlikely that it will be able to catch prey away from water.

Characteristics From its outward appearance, the common caiman could easily be mistaken for a small crocodile. Most animals do not exceed 8 feet (2.5 m) in length though individuals exceeding 10 feet (3 m) have been reported. It is heavily armored along its back.

Diet Smaller animals eat mainly insects, crabs and other invertebrates, while larger individuals eat water snails and fish.

Reproduction The common caiman carefully constructs a mound nest out of soil, leaf litter and fresh vegetation. The nest is usually hidden among bushes or trees though some are made in open fields or on the floating grass mats that cover the shallow parts of large lakes. Females lay 15–40 eggs, depending on the size of the animal, and stay near the nests to defend them against predators. They remain with the hatchlings at least during the first

few weeks of life, but if the level of the water drops markedly, they will abandon the young in search of deeper pools.

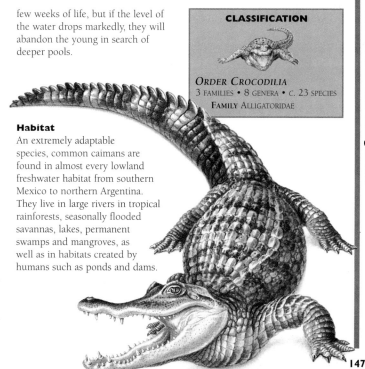

CLASSIFICATION

ORDER CROCODILIA
3 FAMILIES • 8 GENERA • C. 23 SPECIES
FAMILY ALLIGATORIDAE

Habitat
An extremely adaptable species, common caimans are found in almost every lowland freshwater habitat from southern Mexico to northern Argentina. They live in large rivers in tropical rainforests, seasonally flooded savannas, lakes, permanent swamps and mangroves, as well as in habitats created by humans such as ponds and dams.

147

CHARACTERISTICS

Crocodilians are stealthy hunters. Lying submerged, with only their eyes, ears and nostrils showing, they drift slowly toward their prey, attacking with a sudden rush and surprising the fish swimming unawares or the antelope drinking at the water's edge.

Snouts
Crocodilian snouts vary in shape and size according to their diet and the way they live. Long slender snouts, for example, are useful for poking into burrows to find crabs. Species with shorter, wider snouts catch larger prey.

Teeth Crocodilians have many conical teeth which they lose constantly when they hunt. New teeth grow to replace the damaged and missing ones. Their teeth are designed to grip, not cut and chew, so crocodilians swallow their prey whole or tear it into large pieces by twisting and spinning their bodies.

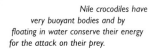

Nile crocodiles have very buoyant bodies and by floating in water conserve their energy for the attack on their prey.

AQUATIC ADAPTATIONS

A crocodilian can breathe while almost totally submerged as it has nostrils on top of its snout that remain above the water. It also has a throat flap that stops water entering the windpipe when the animal is struggling with prey under the water.

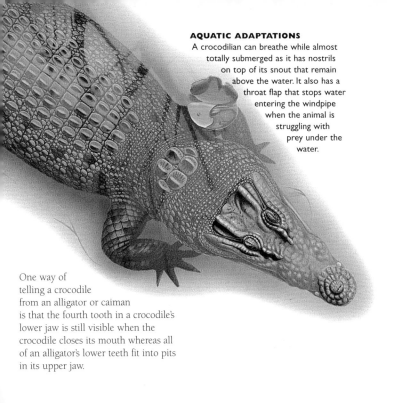

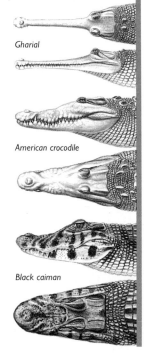

Gharial

American crocodile

Black caiman

One way of telling a crocodile from an alligator or caiman is that the fourth tooth in a crocodile's lower jaw is still visible when the crocodile closes its mouth whereas all of an alligator's lower teeth fit into pits in its upper jaw.

NILE CROCODILE

The Nile crocodile *Crocodylus niloticus* is the biggest and strongest freshwater predator in Africa. When lying motionless in water, its coloring makes it difficult to detect. It often conceals itself even more by floating next to reeds or under an overhanging tree. From this sit-and-wait position, it will make a powerful lunge at an unsuspecting animal approaching the water's edge. If it detects prey when some distance from shore, the crocodile will swim underwater until it is close, surfacing once or twice to check the location of the prey. Its final lunge make take the crocodile several times its own length up the river bank.

LITTLE TO FEAR

The Nile crocodile has no enemies apart from hippopotamuses, which probably only attack in defense of their calves, and other crocodiles and humans. Crocodiles that have come onto land at night have sometimes been attacked by lions.

BASKING AND BATHING

Like many crocodilians, Nile crocodiles regulate their temperature by their behavior. Much of the Nile crocodile's day is spent basking on the river bank. If they become too hot they cool down by opening their mouth to let moisture evaporate. When the air temperature drops, they slip back into the water where it is warmer.

Characteristics The Nile crocodile grows to 18 feet (5.5 m). It has a broad, pointed snout and its skin is shades of drab green, brown and black with adults being uniformly dark.

Diet Young Nile crocodiles eat insects, spiders and frogs. Adults eat anything from fish and birds to antelopes, zebras and humans. Large adults have been seen taking fully grown Cape buffaloes. They kill big animals by dragging them into the water and drowning them.

Reproduction The female digs a flask-shaped hole in the ground, far enough from water to avoid potential flooding. She lays 50–80 eggs and covers them with soil.

Habitat Nile crocodiles live in a variety of freshwater habitats—rivers, streams, lagoons, lakes, swamps— and occasionally at the mouths of rivers and on beaches. The are found in Africa and Madagascar.

CLASSIFICATION

ORDER CROCODILIA
3 FAMILIES • 8 GENERA • C. 23 SPECIES
FAMILY CROCODYLIDAE

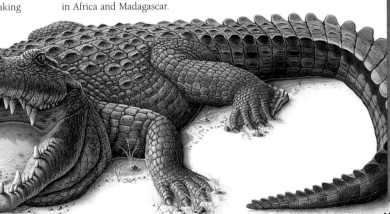

INDOPACIFIC CROCODILE

There are few more dangerous or formidable predators than a large crocodile, and the largest and probably most feared of them all is the Indopacific or saltwater crocodile *Crocodylus porosus*. The Indopacific crocodile is the only crocodile to enter the sea and it has been seen swimming in the ocean 620 miles (1,000 km) from land. On the crocodile's tongue are glands that secrete excess salt, allowing it to survive in a marine environment.

CLASSIFICATION

ORDER CROCODILIA
3 FAMILIES • 8 GENERA • C. 23 SPECIES
FAMILY CROCODYLIDAE

Characteristics The crocodile has a heavy elongated snout. Lengths of more than 23 feet (7 m) and weights of nearly a ton (1,000 kg) have been recorded for males. Females reach 13 feet (4 m). Its coloring varies. Juveniles are brightly patterned with black blotches or bands. Adults may be dark brown, gray or golden tan, and some retain the black markings.

Diet Juveniles eat insects, crabs, shrimps, lizards, mudskippers and snakes. Adults eat fish, birds and whatever mammals they can catch.

Reproduction The females build mound nests during the wet season and lay clutches of 60–80 eggs.

Habitat The crocodile occurs in the sea and in the estuaries and mouths of large rivers as well as in freshwater rivers and lakes. Its range extends from India to northern Australia and the Solomon Islands.

JOHNSTON'S CROCODILE

Although once feared, Johnston's crocodile *Crocodylus johnsoni* of tropical Australia is now usually considered harmless to humans. A slender-snouted crocodile, it is interested in much smaller prey. It is usually sighted basking on the bank or in the shallows at the water's edge, where it catches its food, but at the slightest disturbance it dives and swims out to deeper water.

CLASSIFICATION

ORDER CROCODILIA
3 FAMILIES • 8 GENERA • C. 23 SPECIES
FAMILY CROCODYLIDAE

Characteristics This small species rarely exceeds 10 feet (3 m) in length. It is usually brown in color with black bands on the tail and irregular, darker bands on the body.

Diet Like most crocodilians, this species is an opportunistic feeder. It eats insects, crustaceans, spiders, fish, frogs, lizards, snakes, birds, and small mammals like rats and bats.

Reproduction In the dry season, when there is no danger of flooding, the female excavates a hole nest in a somewhat exposed area such as the sand of a dry river bed. The hole goes down about 20 inches (50 cm) to where the earth is damp. There is relatively little parental defense of the nest and more than half of the dozen or so eggs laid will fall victim to nest robbers, mainly goannas.

Habitat This crocodile inhabits the upper reaches of rivers, and billabongs and swamps in tropical northern Australia. Habitat size varies with the season: it may be extensive in the wet when large areas are flooded, but limited in the dry to isolated deep pools.

LOCOMOTION

Crocodilians spend much of their lives lying motionless on river banks or floating lazily in water, but when prey presents itself or the crocodilian is threatened or disturbed, it can erupt into swift and sudden movement.

CROCODILE WALK
Crocodiles crawl or slither on their bellies for short distances, especially when they enter the water from a river bank and do not want to alert prey by disturbing the water's surface. On dry land, they lift their bodies off the ground and walk, dragging their tails.

Excellent swimmers All the crocodilians move gracefully and with ease in water. They swim with sideways S-shaped strokes of their muscular tail, which propels the body through the water. This type of locomotion must be very efficient because crocodiles have been seen at sea hundreds of miles from land. Crocodilians generally cruise slowly with a gentle sweeping motion of the tail and with their limbs held against

the body. However, when chasing prey or escaping danger, they can move quite rapidly, even leaping out of the water in a "tail walk" reminiscent of dolphins. The sudden lunge of a crocodile to snap at a bird in an overhanging branch can lift it almost entirely out of the water. The tail also powers the thrust of a large crocodile as it explodes out of the water to take a mammal that has ventured too close to the bank.

Calm waters Despite their excellent swimming abilities, crocodilians usually avoid areas with strong wind and wave action. In calm water the animal needs to keep

crocodile crawl

only the tip of its snout above the water, so it can breathe. In rough water the snout has to be raised at a steep angle above the water, which makes swimming more difficult. While floating quietly on the lookout for prey, crocodiles use their fore- and hindlimbs to tread water.

On land A crocodilian's tail is useless on land where it must rely on its short legs for locomotion. When they need to move rapidly, usually to retreat to water, they use a sprawling, awkward gait. On slippery or muddy surfaces they will slide or crawl on their bellies. For long-distance or more leisurely movements over dry land, crocodilians use a "high walk" similar to that of a walking mammal,

A Nile crocodile out for a walk.

with the legs positioned almost vertically under the body and the belly held well off the ground. Small species, and young animals of larger species, can gallop at speeds ranging from 2 to 11 miles per hour (3–18 km/hr) but only for short distances as they become totally exhausted by the effort.

AT A GALLOP
The most spectacular crocodilian gait is that of Johnston's crocodile. To escape back to water over short distances, it gallops, using the same stride sequence as a horse at high speed. The hindlimbs propel the body forward and high off the ground. If fact, all four limbs may be off the ground at the same time.

crocodile walk

crocodile gallop

155

AFRICAN SLENDER-SNOUTED CROCODILE

This crocodile *Crocodylus cataphractus* has a unique way of catching fish. It swims slowly, parallel to the river bank with its tail curved toward the bank. Fish in the shallows move ahead of the disturbance and are trapped when the crocodile turns its head toward the bank, seizing the fish with a sideways sweep of its open jaws.

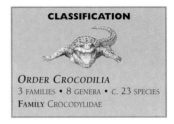

CLASSIFICATION

ORDER CROCODILIA
3 FAMILIES • 8 GENERA • C. 23 SPECIES
FAMILY CROCODYLIDAE

Characteristics The crocodile grows to 10–13 feet (3–4 m) in length. It is quite noisy when vocalizing. It roars repeatedly, sounding like a truck exhaust backfiring.

Diet The slender snout of the crocodile is too fragile to take large prey on land but is equipped with teeth that can subdue quite substantial fish in water. As well as fish, the diet of this crocodile includes insects, shrimps and other crustaceans, crabs, frogs and snakes.

Reproduction The crocodile builds a mound nest out of vegetation along the banks of small rainforest streams. The dense canopy prevents sunlight reaching the nest, so heat from the rotting vegetation keeps the eggs warm. About 13–27 eggs are laid.

Habitat The African slender-snouted crocodile inhabits the heavily forested areas of West and Central Africa.

DWARF CROCODILE

The tiny dwarf crocodile *Osteolaemus tetraspis* of West Africa is a docile, timid, nocturnal creature. It is rarely seen during the day and does not spend long periods basking in the open like many other crocodiles. Little is known of its life history, but because it lives in a similar heavily forested habitat and looks rather like them, it is possible the crocodile has a similar ecology to the dwarf caimans of South America's Amazon basin.

CLASSIFICATION

ORDER CROCODILIA
3 FAMILIES • 8 GENERA • C. 23 SPECIES
FAMILY CROCODYLIDAE

Characteristics The dwarf crocodile rarely exceeds 6½ feet (2 m) in length and averages around 5 feet (1.5 m). It is heavily armored all over its body, even its eyelids, a factor that, along with its small size, has helped to save it from the intense exploitation suffered by the Nile crocodile. Juveniles are dark brown with black and yellow markings. The adults are uniformly dark. The crocodile has brown eyes.

Diet Fish, frogs and crabs make up the major part of the crocodile's diet.

Reproduction Little is known about the life history of this crocodile but in captivity it has been observed building a mound nest and laying clutches of fewer than 20 eggs.

Habitat The dwarf crocodile lives in the rainforests and savannas of tropical West and Central Africa. It seems to prefer slow-moving water and avoids major waterways.

AMERICAN CROCODILE

All crocodilians vocalize to some extent but the American crocodile *Crocodylus acutus* calls infrequently, relying more on visual cues for communication and on a behavior known as headslapping. The headslap is performed by lifting the head so the lower jaw is just above the surface of the water. The crocodile then swiftly opens and closes its mouth, producing a sound similar to that made by slapping a flat shovel on water. Most species perform one headslap at a time, but a territorial American crocodile will advertise his dominance by headslapping the water two or three times in succession.

Characteristics The average length of an American crocodile is 13 feet (4 m) but they have been known to exceed 20 feet (6 m). Juveniles are light in color, usually yellowish tan to gray, with black markings which fade as the animal grows older. Adults are olive-brown or tan with some populations being darker. Its neck is less heavily armored than most crocodiles.

Diet The hatchlings eat insects and the juveniles eat fish, aquatic invertebrates, frogs, turtles, birds and small mammals. Adult animals eat all

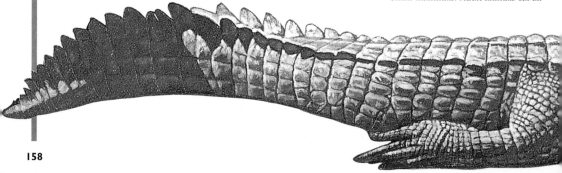

the same things as the younger animals along with larger mammals and birds.

Reproduction The American crocodile is the only crocodilian that builds both mound and hole nests. Usually it buries its eggs in holes in sand or river banks but if a suitable nesting site is not available it will sometimes make a mound, of sand or vegetation, in which to place the eggs. The female lays up to 40 eggs. The adults remain near the nests, in burrows in the river bank which are 10–30 feet (3–9 m) long, and appear to guard them.

Habitat The American crocodile is the only crocodilian widespread in the Americas. Its range extends from the southern tip of Florida in the USA, through the Caribbean Islands, and along the coasts of Central America to the northern coast of South America. It usually lives in coastal habitats such as estuaries and mangroves but can also be found upstream in rivers and large lakes. Although it is not considered a marine animal, it has been sighted far out to sea.

CLASSIFICATION

ORDER CROCODILIA
3 FAMILIES • 8 GENERA • C. 23 SPECIES
FAMILY CROCODYLIDAE

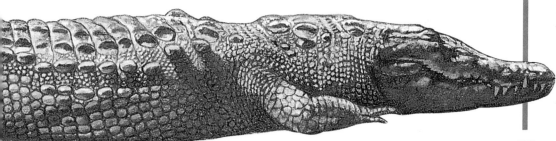

GHARIAL

One of the most distinctive crocodilians, the gharial *Gavialis gangeticus* gets its name from the knob on the tip of the male's snout, called a "ghara," meaning "pot" in Hindi. Air snorted through the nostrils in the knob produces a buzzing noise that warns other males away. The gharial spends more time in water than most other crocodilians and its long narrow snout and many small pointed teeth are ideal for grasping slippery fish.

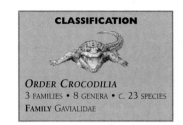

CLASSIFICATION

ORDER CROCODILIA
3 FAMILIES • 8 GENERA • C. 23 SPECIES
FAMILY GAVIALIDAE

Characteristics
The thin-snouted head and weak legs of the gharial seem disproportionately small in relation to its large body. Gharials grow to lengths of 20 feet (6 m).

Diet
Fish are the main food of the gharial but it also eats insects, frogs and other small animals.

Reproduction
The average clutch of a gharial varies from 28 to 43 eggs, depending on the locality. It digs hole nests in sandy river banks or on mid-river islands.

Habitat
The gharial lives in fast-flowing rivers and hill streams in India, Pakistan, Bangladesh, Nepal, Bhutan and Burma.

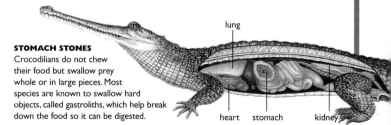

STOMACH STONES
Crocodilians do not chew their food but swallow prey whole or in large pieces. Most species are known to swallow hard objects, called gastroliths, which help break down the food so it can be digested.

lung

heart   stomach   kidney

FALSE GHARIAL

Like other slender-snouted crocodilians, the false or Malayan gharial *Tomistoma schlegelii* catches fish with a sweeping sideways snap. This crocodilian was called the "false" gharial because although it resembled the Indian gharial it was considered to have evolved as part of the crocodile family. Recent biochemical studies, however, have placed the false gharial in the same family as the Indian gharial.

Characteristics This is quite a large species, reaching lengths of 13 feet (4 m) or more. It is distinctively marked with dark bands and blotches, and is one of the few species where the adults are almost as colorful as the juveniles.

Diet The false gharial is mainly a fish-eater but it also feeds on small vertebrates such as frogs, lizards, snakes and water birds.

Reproduction The female builds a mound nest out of vegetation. She lays between 20 and 60 eggs in the dry season and the hatchlings appear at the beginning of the wet season 10 or 12 weeks later. Many of the eggs are eaten by lizards and wild pigs.

Habitat The false gharial inhabits freshwater swamps, lakes and rivers. It occurs on the Malay Peninsula of Thailand and Malaysia, and on the islands of Sumatra, Java, Borneo and possibly Sulawesi.

CLASSIFICATION

ORDER CROCODILIA
3 FAMILIES • 8 GENERA • C. 23 SPECIES
FAMILY GAVIALIDAE

The false gharial was long thought to be a member of the Crocodylidae family. Its thin snout is an adaptation to a diet of largely fish.

MATERNAL CARE

Crocodilians may be ferocious predators, but the females, sometimes with a little help from dad, look after their eggs and young more carefully than most reptiles. This is essential if the young are to survive, as both the eggs and hatchlings are preyed on by a huge number of other animals, including humans.

Hatchlings utter loud grunts, yelps and croaks to attract their mother's attention.

Guarding the nest

Some crocodilians make nests by scraping soil and vegetation into mounds; others bury their eggs in holes dug in sand or soil. The eggs take 60 to 100 days to develop, depending on the species and the temperature of the nest. During this time, the mother, and sometimes the father, will remain near the nest to defend it against predators. Some species rarely leave the nest except to drink at nearby

SALTWATER GUARDIAN

For the 100 days her eggs take to incubate, the Indopacific crocodile rarely goes far from her nest. She will attack any intruder that comes close. Sometimes she digs out a wallow which fills with water just beside her nest where she can lie on guard but unseen.

pools. Others may stay only for the early days of incubation when the fresh nest is easy to detect. Others pay regular nightly visits.

Help at hatching When the hatchlings first break through the shell they begin calling from within the nest. In response to this, the mother scrapes a hole in the nest to release them. Often roots or termite workings will have completely encased the eggs, so without help from the parent the babies could not escape from the nest. Once the hatchlings are free of the nest, the mother in many species gently

picks them up in her mouth and carries them to water, often a quiet pool overhung with reeds and grass. The Nile crocodile even picks up the unhatched eggs, gently rolling them between her tongue and palate until the shell breaks.

Caring for the young The mother, and sometimes other adults, guard the babies in groups for periods ranging from a few weeks to years in the case of some American alligators. One of the safest places for a young crocodilian is on its mother's back or head. Here they can bask or rest secure from attack.

An American alligator carries her newly hatched babies to a quiet pond.

TUATARAS

Tuataras are the only living member of the order Rhynchocephalia. Rhynchocephalians were small to medium-sized reptiles common throughout the world between about 225 and 120 million years ago, long before the first dinosaurs appeared. Later their numbers declined and about 60 million years ago they became extinct everywhere except New Zealand. Tuataras are often called "living fossils" but recent research suggests they have much more advanced features than their nearest extinct relatives. Once regarded as a single species, *Sphenodon punctatus*, scientists now believe the tuataras on North Brother Island are different enough to be regarded as a separate species, *Sphenodon guntheri*.

TUATARAS

Tuataras are active mostly at night when they come out to hunt. They spend the day in burrows or, if it is sunny, basking at the burrow entrance. There are no ponds or streams on the islands where the tuataras live so after dry spells they are particularly active on rainy nights when they may often be found soaking in puddles. For hunting, tuataras usually adopt a sit and wait strategy. When small prey items come close they are first seized with the tongue. Larger animals are impaled on the tuatara's sharp teeth.

BIGGER AND SPIKIER
When the Maoris first saw this unusual reptile, they called it "tuatara" meaning "lightning back." This refers to the crest of large spikes on the male's back. The male (bottom) has larger spines on its back and neck than the female, and is heavier and larger. Males weigh over 2 lb (1 kg), which is double that of a female. Males can grow to 2 ft (60 cm) in length, females to 1½ ft (45 cm).

Characteristics Tuataras are gray, olive green or occasionally rusty red. While they resemble lizards, they are quite different. For example, they have no external ears, their teeth are fused to the jaw and they have no penis, whereas lizards have two. Tuataras have a "third eye," part of an organ on top of the brain. It has a lens, retina and nerve connection to the brain, but early in the growth of the tuatara it is covered by opaque scales. Many lizards also have a "third eye" which is involved in regulating temperature, but it is not known what function, if any, a tuatara's "third eye" performs.

Diet Insects, snails and earthworms make up the bulk of the tuatara's diet. They also eat lizards, and small birds and their eggs.

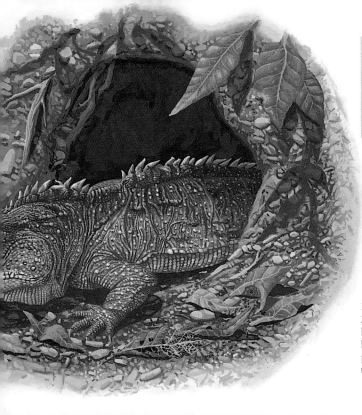

Reproduction Tuataras mate by touching cloacae. The females gather in an open sunny spot to dig nests in the soil where they lay an average of eight eggs. Females guard their nests for about a week to prevent other females digging up the same site. The incubation period of 12 to 15 months is one of the longest of any reptile.

Habitat Tuataras are found on 30 small islands off the coast of New Zealand. Some are forested, others have stunted vegetation. They live in burrows that have been built by the petrels which share their habitat, or they excavate their own.

LIZARDS

No other group of reptiles has evolved into as many different forms as the lizards. They range from tiny legless worm-like creatures to giant monitors with powerful limbs. They come in all colors, from drab browns and grays to bright pinks, blues and greens. All lizards are covered with scales that stop them from drying out in the heat, yet some have rough, spiky skin with crests and horns, others have smooth, sleek bodies. They eat mainly insects and other invertebrates, which they crush with their sharp, pointed teeth, but some lizards eat plants and flowers and the Komodo dragon, the largest of all lizards, can kill and eat a water buffalo.

TREE DRAGON

The astonishingly slender tree dragon *Diporiphora superba*, one of the world's most slender agamids, has a tail that is three to four times its body length. It has only been known to science since 1974 and lives in the foliage of the acacia trees in north-west Australia. When still, its green coloring and thin, almost stick-like, body and limbs make it nearly invisible among the narrow leaves.

THIN AND AGILE
The long, whip-like tail of the tree dragon is its most distinctive characteristic. The tree dragon, being so recently discovered, has been little studied.

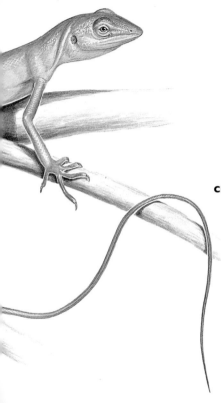

CLASSIFICATION

Order Squamata
suborder Sauria
26 families
420 genera • 4,300 species
Family Agamidae

Characteristics The tree dragon has a slender body around 3.5 inches (9 cm) in length, and a long tail, limbs and toes. Its color ranges from pale lime green to a greenish yellow. Like all agamid lizards, its tail has no fracture planes and is never shed. It is agile and escapes from predators using its speed, agility and brilliant camouflage.

Diet The diet of the tree dragon consists primarily of insects and spiders.

Reproduction Like other members of its group, the tree dragon lays eggs, probably in a clutch of between two and four. Its preferred egg-laying site is unknown.

Habitat The tree dragon lives almost exclusively in acacia trees. It is found in the hot sandstone plateau regions of north-western Western Australia.

173

MILITARY DRAGON

The military dragon *Ctenophorus isolepis* is widespread in the very dry regions of Australia. It can move extremely quickly and if threatened or pursued will run swiftly across open ground, relying on speed rather than seeking cover to escape. During the summer, when temperatures are high, it is active in the early morning and late afternoon. In winter it is active in the middle of the day.

CLASSIFICATION

ORDER SQUAMATA
SUBORDER SAURIA • 26 FAMILIES
420 GENERA • 4,300 SPECIES
FAMILY AGAMIDAE

Characteristics

The females of this beautifully marked, rather small species are slightly larger than the males with average body lengths of 2½ inches (6.5 cm) and 2 inches (6 cm) respectively. They have long limbs and a long slender tail.

Diet The diet of the military dragon consists mostly of ants, which it actively hunts, though it occasionally eats other small arthropods and small lizards.

Reproduction Two or three clutches of one to six eggs are laid in the spring and summer. The eggs take around two months to hatch.

Habitat This ground-dwelling lizard inhabits Australian sandplain and dunefield deserts—which cover nearly half of inland Australia—especially those areas dominated by spinifex, which it uses for shelter.

FRILL-NECKED LIZARD

When threatened, the frill-necked lizard *Chlamydosaurus kingii* usually tries to escape by running swiftly on its powerful hind legs, its body erect and its very long tail acting as a counterbalance. However if the lizard feels cornered, it will resort to a spectacular display of bluff. Facing its attacker, it raises the front of its body, extends its enormous frill and hisses loudly through its wide open mouth.

CLASSIFICATION

ORDER SQUAMATA
SUBORDER SAURIA • 26 FAMILIES
420 GENERA • 4,300 SPECIES
FAMILY AGAMIDAE

Characteristics With a body length of about 9 inches (23 cm), this lizard is Australia's largest agamid. Colorful areas of red, yellow and orange are revealed when its frill is extended, but when folded it disrupts the body's outline and this, along with the lizard's dull gray or brown coloring, provides it with camouflage. There are many blood vessels in the frill, so it is thought that it may also be used to regulate body temperature. Extending the frill in the sun could increase the rate at which the lizard's temperature rises.

Diet The lizard's diet consists of large insects like grasshoppers and beetles, plus spiders and small mammals such as mice.

Reproduction Between nine and 12 eggs are laid in a nesting burrow. They hatch in eight to 12 weeks.

Habitat The lizard spends most its time in trees where its coloration enables it to blend in with the trunks and boughs on which it rests. It is found in open forests and woodlands across northern Australia.

AFRICAN AGAMA LIZARDS

There are not many agamid lizards in Africa, but those belonging to the genus *Agama* are the most common and they are very conspicuous. The males of all species are brightly colored and during the breeding season they intensify or change these colors for courtship and territorial displays. Many have a brightly colored head which they bob rapidly up and down when seeking a mate.

DIFFERENT COLORS
As with many other agamids, there is a marked color difference between the sexes of the African agama lizards. Males are deep blue or purple with an orange or red head and tail. Females and juveniles are less brightly colored, with brownish or grayish bodies with yellow marks on the head and orange spots on the shoulders.

Characteristics These spiny lizards vary in length from 5 to 12 inches (13–30 cm), with the males being larger than the females. The lizards are extremely active during much of the day, darting about the ground looking for ants, or leaping into the air to snap up flying insects. They retreat to cool shady spots only when the temperature reaches about 100°F (38°C). They come out to hunt again when the temperature drops in the late afternoon.

Diet Insects make up the main part of the African agama lizards' diet, but they also eat grass, berries and seeds, and the eggs of smaller lizards.

Reproduction Each brightly colored male has a territory which he defends vigorously against other males, and he mates with a number of females. When a male catches sight of a rival he will repeatedly raise and lower the front part of his body in a jerky bobbing action, and he may also lash out with his strong tail. Mating and egg-laying take place after the rainy season when the vegetation is lush and the insect populations rise. The female lays a clutch of around 12 eggs.

Habitat There are several tree-dwelling African agama lizards but most species live among rocks and boulders where they spend much of their time basking in the sun and displaying to other members of their species. A few species retreat to burrows to escape from predators or to avoid very high temperatures. The lizards are found all over Africa, south of the Sahara Desert.

CLASSIFICATION

ORDER *SQUAMATA*
SUBORDER *SAURIA* • 26 FAMILIES
420 GENERA • 4,300 SPECIES
FAMILY *AGAMIDAE*

A BRIGHT MESSAGE
Only the mature, dominant males like this agama lizard have bright orange and blue coloring. Weak, subordinate males or immature males are various shades of brown in color. Even a male that gets a fright can go brown, and they all—even the dominant males—lose their gaudy hues overnight. When they re-emerge into the early morning sun, the bright colors return.

CHUCKWALLAS

The chuckwallas are stocky, terrestrial lizards that live in American desert regions. When threatened, a chuckwalla will seek refuge in a rocky crevice into which it will wedge itself tightly by inflating its body with gulps of air. These lizards emerge in the early morning and bask in the sun until their optimum body temperature is reached. Then they begin searching for food.

CLASSIFICATION

ORDER SQUAMATA
SUBORDER SAURIA • 26 FAMILIES
420 GENERA • 4,300 SPECIES
FAMILY IGUANIDAE

Characteristics These large, bulky lizards have loose folds of skin on their neck and sides. They reach body lengths of up to 8 inches (20 cm). Their thick tail is about the same length. They can change their skin color from dark to light to reflect or absorb heat from the sun.

Diet Chuckwallas are herbivorous. They eat flowers, leaves, buds and fruit, including the fruit of cactus.

Reproduction The males use a combination of head-bobbing, push-ups and mouth displays to attract a mate and to establish their territory. Five to 10 eggs are laid in the summer.

Habitat Chuckwallas live on rocky outcrops and hillsides in the deserts of southern USA, Mexico and the islands of Baja California.

The piebald chuckwalla
Sauromalus varius is
found on San Estaban
Island in the Gulf of
California.

SAIL-TAILED WATER LIZARD

The large, semi-aquatic sail-tailed lizard *Hydrosaurus amboinensis*, also known as the soasoa or water dragon, basks on rocks and branches at the edge of streams, retreating to the water when in danger. Aided by fringes on the toes of its hind feet, it can run on the surface of the water for some distance before sinking and swimming away.

CLASSIFICATION

ORDER SQUAMATA
SUBORDER SAURIA • 26 FAMILIES
420 GENERA • 4,300 SPECIES
FAMILY AGAMIDAE

Characteristics The stocky sail-tailed water lizard is the largest lizard in the agamid family with a total length of over 3 feet (1 m). Its strong, compressed tail and toe fringes increase its surface area to increase swimming efficiency. It moves swiftly and effortlessly through the water, using its feet and its flattened, paddle-like tail.

Diet This lizard is an ambush predator, preying on a variety of small invertebrates.

Reproduction Like most agamid lizards, this species is oviparous.

Habitat This semi-arboreal lizard is a tree-dweller that lives in close association with streams and rivers in Indonesia and New Guinea.

CHAMELEONS

This very distinctive family of lizards are famous for their ability to change color. This trait is shared with many other lizards, but is particularly well developed in the chameleons. Changing color helps these lizards to blend in with their surroundings, a feature that is useful for stalking prey as well as for hiding from enemies. Color change is also associated with sexual and territorial displays and with temperature.

Characteristics Chameleons, even the ground-dwelling species, are built for living in trees. On each foot they have two sets of opposed, partly fused toes used for gripping twigs and narrow branches in a pincer action. Their prehensile tail acts as a fifth limb when climbing. They have turret-like eyes that can be moved independently of each other, so they have excellent depth perception, necessary for aiming their extremely long tongue and for judging distance in dense vegetation.

Diet Most chameleons eat insects, spiders and scorpions, though the larger species will prey on small birds and mammals.

SOUND THE HORN

Jackson's chameleon *Chamaeleo jacksonii* of Africa is one of several species in which the males possess horns or other appendages on the head that play a role in species recognition between the sexes and which may be used in intense combat among the males.

The flap-necked chameleon Chamaeleo dilepis *is the most widespread chameleon in southern Africa.*

Reproduction Some chameleons, including the dwarf chameleons, give birth to live young several times a year. The young are born in a translucent membrane which they soon struggle out of. Most species lay eggs, however, with the number per clutch largely dependent on body size. One of the largest, Meller's chameleon, lays up to 70 eggs, and clutches of 30 to 40 are the rule for many species. Females usually bury the eggs in the ground or in rotting logs or other moist, protected spots.

Habitat Most chameleons live in trees in humid forest areas, and they are especially numerous in the rainforest belt of eastern Madagascar and the highland forests of East Africa and the Cameroons. However they are also successful in some Mediterranean climates and even in deserts. Not all are arboreal. The arid-zone species, such as the Namaqua chameleon of south-west Africa, spend most of their time on the ground, as do the stump-tailed chameleons of Madagascar.

The Fisher chameleon Chamaeleo fischeri *is a species from equatorial Africa. The region is home to numerous species.*

TONGUES AND TAILS

Lizards have developed special features to suit their different habitats. For example, all lizards have external ear openings but those that live beneath the ground have a scaly cover over them. In the same way, a lizard's tongue and tail will often reflect its lifestyle.

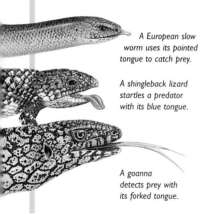

A European slow worm uses its pointed tongue to catch prey.

A shingleback lizard startles a predator with its blue tongue.

A goanna detects prey with its forked tongue.

Forked tongues All lizards have well-developed tongues but they vary greatly in structure. Monitor lizards and whiptails, for example, have slender, deeply forked tongues which, like snakes, they use to "taste" scent particles in the air. These particles are passed by the tongue to small pits in the roof of the mouth and then to sensory cells that connect to the lizard's brain. This is how they detect their prey or sense the presence of an enemy. The beaded lizards also have forked tongues. The gila monster, which hunts mainly for subterranean animals, uses its tongue almost exclusively when tracking prey.

Fleshier models In some lizards, like the geckos and flap-footed lizards, the tongue is fleshier and is used for lapping up water or nectar. Geckos also use their tongue for "spectacle wiping"—cleaning the transparent scale over each eye. Some lizards, such as the Australian blue-tongued and pink-tongued skink, have strikingly colored, flattened tongues which they use to startle predators.

Food catchers Not all lizards use their tongue to grasp food and bring it to the mouth. Those that do include the iguanas and the agamid lizards, but it is the chameleons, with their incredibly long tongues, that have developed this ability to an amazing degree.

A tale in the tail Lizards' tails have many uses. Tree-dwelling chameleons, for example, have prehensile tails that grip twigs and branches and help them to hang on when they are moving about. Some lizards, like the Australian shingle-back and the gila monster, have club-like tails where they store fat for lean times. Many lizards, including skinks, lacertids and geckos, have long streamlined tails that can be shed to escape a predator. Leaf-tailed geckos, which live in rock outcrops or trees, have flattened, camouflaged tails which, like their flattened bodies, allow them to shelter under loose bark or in narrow crevices.

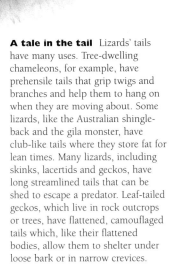

chameleon

leaf-tailed gecko

skink

shingleback

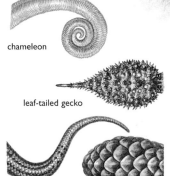

LONG AND STICKY

Chameleons have an incredibly long tongue which they use with great speed and efficiency to catch their insect prey. They move slowly toward their prey and shoot out their tongue, which is covered in sticky mucus that traps the insect. They then draw the tongue rapidly back into the mouth. The tip of the tongue often exceeds speeds of 16 feet (5 m) per second as it travels toward the unsuspecting insect.

GREEN IGUANA

The green, or common, iguana *Iguana iguana* is the largest South American lizard. Essentially arboreal, the lizard is never found far from trees. It is an agile climber and can scramble from tree to tree if the foliage is interlaced enough to support it. Like the sail-tailed water lizard, it sometimes basks on branches overhanging streams and drops into the water if disturbed. It can dive underwater and is a good swimmer, propelling itself through the water with its tail.

Characteristics The crest that runs along the back of the green iguana and resembles the teeth in a comb is a row of enlarged scales. The lizard has sharp claws that it uses to grasp branches and twigs when climbing. Under its throat is a folded dewlap that it can extend to frighten enemies and which males display to attract a female. The males are larger than the females and reach lengths of up to $6\frac{1}{2}$ ft (2 m), including the tail. The color of the lizards varies from grass green to blue-green. In the breeding season, some males develop tinges of orange on their crest and legs. The males

AN ADAPTABLE LIZARD

The green iguana, a highly adaptable species, thrives even in environments that have been disturbed by humans. It is a popular pet in many parts of the world, and is a major source of food for many rural communities. While it is an arboreal species, it is also a speedy runner on land and an efficient swimmer.

claim large territories and warn off intruders by raising their body and nodding their head vigorously. These lizards are fast runners and would rather run that fight. They can throw themselves 40 or 50 feet (12–15 m) to the ground and land unhurt. To survive times of famine they store large amounts of fat in their lower jaw and neck.

Diet Young iguanas eat insects and snails but they become almost totally herbivorous as adults when they eat fruit, leaves, flowers, young shoots and grasses.

Reproduction The females build a long burrow in sandy soil where they bury their eggs. The large clutches of between 20 and 70 eggs take about three months to hatch. The temperature of the nest must remain constant for the eggs to develop. The hatchlings, which are about 10 inches (25 cm) long, all emerge from the nest together,

a strategy that provides safety for individuals against predators. The young iguanas often remain in groups for a short time and sleep together on a tree branch.

Habitat The green iguana inhabits tropical forests in Central and South America, and on Trinidad and Tobago as well as on several of the smaller West Indian islands.

CLASSIFICATION

ORDER SQUAMATA
SUBORDER SAURIA • 26 FAMILIES
420 GENERA • 4,300 SPECIES
FAMILY IGUANIDAE

The comb-like crest is one of the green iguana's most distinctive features.

A UNIQUE MARINE HABITAT

A harsh environment of torrid rock and cold seas, the shores of the Galapagos Islands harbor a wealth of wildlife found nowhere else in the world. Among these extraordinary species are the Galapagos marine iguanas.

SPECIES EVOLUTION

The reason that marine iguanas evolved in Galapagos and are found only there is speculative, but is likely to be explained by several factors. Firstly, much of the coastline is desolate and arid but food can be found at the shoreline. Secondly, conditions for a marine lifestyle are particularly suitable in this unusual tropical location, where a cool marine climate promotes rich algal growth. Lastly, the absence of native, land-based predators has allowed the iguana to survive in an otherwise vulnerable environment.

186

MARINE IGUANA

The marine iguana *Amblyrhynchus cristatus* is the only lizard to venture into the sea where it feeds on marine algae. Most of the iguanas, including the females and the young, feed in the shallow water close to the rocky shore, but the larger males swim further out and dive deep down under the water. An average dive lasts for five to 10 minutes, though the lizards can stay under for much longer, and they can go to depths of 40 feet (12 m) or more.

BLACK BASKER
Although the Galapagos Islands straddle the equator, there is a cold undercurrent in the water that causes the body temperature of the marine iguana to drop markedly while submerged. It therefore spends much of its time basking on the rocks to warm up. The lizard's black skin helps it absorb heat more rapidly.

Characteristics The iguana has a number of adaptations to suit its marine lifestyle. To rid itself of excess salt ingested when feeding, it excretes concentrated salt crystals from a nasal gland. It does this by sneezing frequently when it is back on land, which is why the iguanas often have salt-encrusted heads. Its flattened, paddle-like tail helps the marine iguana when swimming. Marine iguanas have a blunt snout, a stocky body and a crest that runs from the neck to the tail. They grow to about 4 feet (1.2 m) in length.

Diet The marine iguana grazes on the sea bed, feeding almost exclusively on marine algae and seaweed, but it also eats other marine plants, crustaceans, grasshoppers and, occasionally, a sea lion afterbirth.

Reproduction After mating the females travel from the rocky lava reefs to the nesting beaches, a distance of 300 feet (100 m). Here they each scrape out a tunnel in the sand, about 2 feet (60 cm) long, with their feet and lay two or three eggs. The female then covers up the nest and leaves When the young hatch about 16 weeks later, they are about 9 inches (23 cm) long.

Habitat The marine iguana is found throughout the Galapagos Islands. When not foraging for food in the sea, the iguanas can be found basking on the rocks and cliffs beside the shore. There may be thousands at one site, often piled up on one another in large heaps to conserve heat.

CLASSIFICATION

ORDER SQUAMATA
SUBORDER SAURIA • 26 FAMILIES
420 GENERA • 4,300 SPECIES
FAMILY IGUANIDAE

BREEDING DRESS
During the breeding season, the male marine iguana's black skin becomes rusty red and green. Each male claims a territory which he defends vigorously. At first he will threaten a rival by raising the front of his body and bobbing up and down on stiff legs with his red-lined mouth wide open. If this does not deter the intruder then the two competing males will butt their heads together until one gives way and retreats.

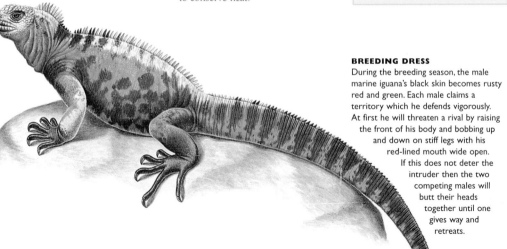

189

ANOLES

Anoles are among the most successful lizards. By adapting to and exploiting all the available microhabitats, large numbers can exist in a single area. Although they are all expert climbers, one species may live in the crown of a tree, one on the tree trunk, and another on the ground below. There may even be further divisions based on size, diet and shade tolerance. In this way the anoles avoid competing with one another for food and other resources.

DEWLAP DISPLAY

Anoles are famous for the colorful sail-like dewlap which the males and the females of some species have on their throat. They display the dewlap to advertise ownership of a territory or to attract a female. The color and shape of the dewlap vary from species to species. Below is a displaying male Cuban brown anole *Anolis sagrei sagrei*.

The knight anole Anolis equestris is a large species from Cuba.

Characteristics Anoles have a long whip-like tail, long legs and a slender body. Their head is triangular in shape with narrow, elongated jaws. They have climbing pads on their long delicate toes, similar to those of the geckos though

not as well developed, as well as sharp claws. Most anoles are small lizards, about 8 inches (20 cm) in total length, though the giant anoles can reach 2 feet (60 cm). Two-thirds of this length is the tail.

Diet The anoles will eat fruit but they are mostly insectivorous with different species preferring different insects. Their diet also changes according to the time of the year and the food available.

Reproduction Nearly all species lay only one egg at a time but most lay a number of times during the breeding season. The female digs a nest in the ground with her feet.

Habitat Most anoles live in trees, but the water anole lives along the banks of streams, and there are two cave-dwelling species as well. They are found in Central and South America, the West Indies, and in south-eastern USA.

CLASSIFICATION

ORDER SQUAMATA
SUBORDER SAURIA • 26 FAMILIES
420 GENERA • 4,300 SPECIES
FAMILY POLYCHROTIDAE

AMERICAN "CHAMELEON"
Anoles like the the green anole *Anolis carolinensis* of North America have the ability to rapidly change color. The color of the green anole ranges from bright green to dark brown. The males have a pink dewlap and the females have a pink throat.

DEFENSE AND ESCAPE

Lizards have many enemies. Spiders, scorpions, other lizards, snakes, birds and mammals all prey on them. Running away or hiding is often the best form of defense and lizards are well known for their speedy escapes, but sometimes this is not possible, so they have developed some extraordinary ways to defend themselves.

Looking scary Some lizards try to frighten attackers by pretending to be bigger or fiercer than they really are. Some lizards extend their neck or throat crest or inflate their neck in order to look bigger. The bearded dragons and frill-necked lizard of Australia have elaborate throat fans which they extend when threatened. Some lizards have brightly colored throats or tongues that they display

When attacked, an Australian bearded dragon will open its yellow mouth wide and display its elaborate throat fan.

BOO!
The frill-necked lizard startles a predator by opening its mouth, hissing loudly and extending the frill behind its neck. The slow-moving blue-tongued skink puffs itself up, sticks out its bright blue tongue and hisses at its attacker.

to startle a predator. Monitors puff their throats out and rear up on their hind legs to look as big as possible. If they become highly agitated, they will scratch and bite, and lash out with their powerful tail.

Tough and spiky Some lizards have long, spiky scales which make them difficult to swallow. The Australian thorny devil, the African girdle-tailed lizards and the horned lizards of North America are so spiky that predators often avoid them.

Camouflage One of the most effective ways to avoid being eaten is not being seen. Many lizards have patterns and colors that blend in with their background, If they keep very still they can become invisible to a predator. Some lizards are able to change their color and pattern to match their environment. The chameleons are the best at this. In only a few seconds they can change quite dramatically by moving and expanding pigments in the skin.

Shedding tails Many small lizards, especially geckos and skinks, are able to shed their tail if it is grasped by a predator. While the predator is distracted by the wriggling, twitching tail, the lizard escapes. It loses very little blood and a new tail grows back over the next few months.

The long blue tail of the western skink from the USA and Mexico distracts a predator away from its vulnerable head and body.

CAN'T CATCH ME
Many lizards escape an attack by going where their predators can't follow. They climb trees and walls, scuttle into crevices or even, in the case of the basilisks, run across water. The flying gecko of South-East Asia has flaps of skin along its side which allow it to glide from tree to tree to escape predators.

193

HORNED LIZARDS

In the evening, to avoid the cool night air, horned lizards dig themselves into the sand. In the early morning they expose first just their head and then their whole body to the sun. The first few hours of the day are spent basking, often with their body flattened and tilted toward the sun to absorb as much heat as possible. When warm enough, they begin to forage for food. If the ground becomes too hot they will seek shade under a bush.

A BLOOD-LETTING

Some horned lizards, like the regal horned lizard *Phrynosoma solare,* have evolved a bizarre defense against predators. Using special muscles, they restrict blood flow from the head until the mounting pressure bursts tiny blood vessels in and around the eyes, resulting in a spurt of blood that can travel 3 feet (1 m) or more and frighten an attacker.

Characteristics Because of their saucer-shaped body, large head and short tail, these lizards are sometimes called horned "toads." Most species have a row of sharp, backward-pointing scales, or "horns," on the back of the head which are used for defense. Most species also have a row of sharp spines along their tail and sides. They grow to about 6 inches (15 cm) in total length.

Diet All species of horned lizards feed mainly on ants though they will also eat other slow-moving, ground-dwelling insects and spiders. The lizards sit beside ant trails flicking up the ants with their long sticky tongue. Because ants are so small, the lizards eat huge numbers of them.

Reproduction Most species lay eggs, burying them in the sand where they hatch several weeks later. In some species the eggs are retained, and the young are hatched just

The desert horned lizard Phrynosoma platyrhinos *is the most common horned lizard in the American western deserts.*

TINY MOUNTAIN DWELLER

The short-horned lizard *Phrynosoma douglassi* (below) is a tiny lizard, not much bigger than a human hand. It lives at higher altitudes than other horned lizards and gives birth to live young. Like all horned lizards, it buries itself in the fall and spends the winter months hibernating, emerging in the spring when daytime temperatures become high enough.

CLASSIFICATION

ORDER *SQUAMATA*
SUBORDER *SAURIA* • 26 FAMILIES
420 GENERA • 4,300 SPECIES
FAMILY PHRYNOSOMATIDAE

before, during, or shortly after laying. The species that live in cooler areas generally give birth to live young.

Habitat Horned lizards live in dry, sandy environments. Some species inhabit scorchingly hot deserts, others live in mountainous areas, as high as 10,000 feet (930 m). These lizards are found in the arid regions of south-western Canada, western USA and western Mexico.

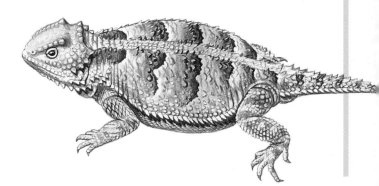

SAND LIZARDS

The sand lizards are well adapted for their life in the hot, dry deserts of North America. Some are able to withstand body temperatures as high as 116°F (47°C). They have very complex posturing behavior which regulates their body temperature. Some sand lizards bury themselves in the loose sand to avoid high temperature and to sleep. They will also dive into the sand to escape from predators.

CLASSIFICATION

ORDER SQUAMATA
SUBORDER SAURIA • 26 FAMILIES
420 GENERA • 4,300 SPECIES
FAMILY PHRYNOSOMATIDAE

The zebra-tailed lizard Callisaurus draconoides is a fast runner and is often seen running on its hind legs.

Characteristics Sand lizards of the genus *Uma* have fringes of enlarged scales on the borders of their toes. These fringes help them to run rapidly across loose sand. These lizards also have valves in their nostrils, flaps over their ears and an upper jaw that overlaps the lower one to prevent sand entering their bodies. A number of sand lizards, like the zebra-tailed lizard, have black and white bands on the underside of their tail. The waving tail mesmerizes a predator, and when the lizard runs off the predator is left staring fixedly at the spot where the waving tail once was.

Diet Sand lizards eat insects, small lizards and, occasionally, blossoms.

Reproduction Small clutches of up to five eggs are laid in summer, probably more than one clutch per season.

Habitat Sand lizards live in the windblown sand dunes and sandy flats in parts of California, Arizona and other arid areas.

FENCE LIZARDS

These widely distributed American lizards are sometimes called spiny lizards because they have pointed scales on their bodies which give them a spiky appearance. Some, like the crevice spiny lizard *Sceloporus poinsetti* (above), have a spiny tail which they use to protect themselves when they retreat into a crack or crevice in their rocky habitats.

CLASSIFICATION

ORDER SQUAMATA
SUBORDER SAURIA • 26 FAMILIES
420 GENERA • 4,300 SPECIES
FAMILY PHRYNOSOMATIDAE

Characteristics Fence lizards vary in size, with total lengths ranging from 1½ to 14 inches (4–35 cm). They have long tails, sometimes one and a half times the head–body length. The females are a drab brown or gray, whereas the males are more brightly colored, especially during the breeding season.

Diet Fence lizards are mostly insectivorous, feeding on a variety of insects, but they will also eat insect larvae and spiders and other arthropods.

Reproduction About 40 percent of the species, usually those that live at higher altitudes, give birth to live young. Most of the lowland species lay eggs.

Habitat Fence lizards occur in a number of habitats. Some live in dry, rocky, desert areas, while others live on the edges of forests or other sunny but not dry regions. Those that live in cooler areas hibernate during the coldest parts of the winter. They occur in south-west USA and Central America.

Eastern fence lizards Sceloporus undulatus *inhabit a wide variety of habitats. Some seek shelter in animal burrows when threatened; others climb trees.*

197

LIVING IN DRY PLACES

Although lizards are found in almost all habitats, they are especially numerous in arid areas. Desert lizards have developed a number of ways to deal with the scorching daytime temperatures and the scarcity of water. Physical adaptations as well as certain ways of behaving allow them to survive where no bird or mammal could.

The gila monster of North America stores fat in its thick tail and can survive without food for several months.

Avoiding the heat Lizards deal with scorching temperatures in different ways. Many species are nocturnal. They hunt in the early evening when the air is cooler but the ground is still warm. Daytime species burrow into cool sand or hide beneath rocks during the hottest part of the day. Some lizards move their bodies in certain ways to minimize the heat absorbed from the sand. The desert fringe-toed lizard, for example, lifts one front leg and the opposite back leg to cool its feet, then swaps to the other legs.

Finding water Most desert lizards get the moisture they need almost entirely from their food. In coastal deserts such as the Namib in Africa and the Atacama in South America, fog from the ocean provides the lizards with water. Others, such as the Asiatic toad-headed agamid and

DUNE DWELLER

The desert plated lizard lives in the sand dunes of the Namib Desert where it forages for insects, plant debris and small desert melons. The rim of its lower jaw is hidden when its mouth is closed to prevent sand entering, and the broad, rectangular fringes on its toes help it move quickly through the sand. When it is disturbed, the lizard dives into the dune and disappears from sight.

CHANNELING RAINWATER

The thorny devil of central Australia, a specialized ant eater, has sharp, spiny scales that are arranged so that they collect rainwater which is then channeled to the mouth via fine grooves.

the Australian thorny devil, catch rainwater in their spines.

Conserving water All lizards are covered with keratin, a substance similar to human fingernails, which prevents water loss through the skin. They also reduce the water lost through excretion, producing droppings that are almost dry. Both adaptations help to conserve water in their arid environment.

BASILISKS

The ability of these lizards to run on the surface of water is the reason for their common name, Jesus lizards. When threatened or in search of food, a basilisk may run quickly toward the water on its two hind legs. This momentary high speed, combined with the fringe of scales on the lizard's toes, which is pushed up when it hits the water, allows it to run on the water for quite some distance before sinking.

CLASSIFICATION

ORDER SQUAMATA
SUBORDER SAURIA • 26 FAMILIES
420 GENERA • 4,300 SPECIES
FAMILY CORYTOPHANIDAE

Characteristics Basilisks are large green or brown lizards with prominent crests and dewlaps and long powerful legs. They can run on their hind legs with their long tails providing counterbalance. They grow to total lengths of up to 3 feet (1 m), much of which is the tail. The females are smaller than the males.

Diet Basilisks feed on invertebrates, especially insects. While juveniles are wholly carnivorous, adults also eat plant matter such as seeds, berries and stems.

Reproduction Basilisks are oviparous, and the numbr of eggs per clutch varies acording to species. Several clutches are laid per season.

Habitat Basilisks live in forested areas on the edges of streams, ponds and lakes. They are found in Central America, from Mexico to Equador.

As well as head ornamentation, the common basilisk Basiliscus basiliscus has a fin-like crest on its back and tail.

MULTI-COLORED TREE LIZARD

The multi-colored tree lizard *Polychrus marmotus* is a rather slow-moving lizard that relies on its camouflage to escape the notice of predators. When it remains motionless, its mottled colors make it almost invisible among the foliage of the shrubs and bushes where it lives. It is mainly active at night Its long tail enables the lizard to balance as it climbs and moves in the forest canopy, and extended toes on its hindlimbs help it to grasp branches.

Characteristics The multi-colored tree lizard and others in its genus are South American relatives of what are popularly known as "false chameleons" in other parts of the Americas. Several species exhibit sexual dimorphism—a marked variation in color between males and females. Males are uniformly dark green to brownish while the females are distinguished by varying patterns of black, white and brown. Like the chameleons, they are able to change color quickly when they are excited or threatened.

Diet These lizards eat a variety of small insects. Little is known about their specific preferences.

Reproduction A clutch of eggs is laid in the ground, where the warmth of the forest litter helps to incubate them.

Habitat This arboreal lizard lives in shrubs and bushes in South America. There are several species of the genus in South America, but each has a restricted range.

201

COLLARED LIZARDS

These lizards are exceptionally fast runners with hearty appetites. When chasing prey, which can be anything from insects to small snakes, collared lizards often run on their hind legs. They are very wary, too, and quick to take cover if startled. They dash across an open space, jump nimbly from rock to rock, or scuttle into a crevice.

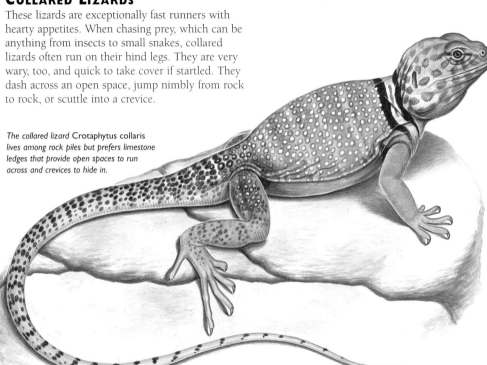

The collared lizard Crotaphytus collaris *lives among rock piles but prefers limestone ledges that provide open spaces to run across and crevices to hide in.*

The distinctive banded head of the collared lizard.

Characteristics Collared lizards have large heads, wide mouths and slender necks. Many have a conspicuous black or black and white collar across the back of the neck. The lizards have long strong limbs and tails. They vary in total length from 6 to 17 inches (15–44 cm). Males and females of the same species are differently colored, with the males often being more vivid during the breeding season. Changes like red or orange spots or bars also appear on the sides of pregnant females.

Diet These predatory lizards prey on small lizards, snakes and mammals. They also eat insects and spiders.

Reproduction These lizards mate between April and July. During the summer months, clutches of eggs are laid in loose sandy soil, in burrows or under rocks. The young, which take around six to eight weeks to hatch, are distinctively marked with bright spots or crossbands which fade they grow older.

Habitat Collared lizards inhabit a range of habitats, from forests to arid or semi-arid areas. They prefer hilly limestone regions that provide crevices and other hiding places for protection. They live and bask on boulders and take shelter under debris, in crevices or in animal burrows.Their distribution ranges fom Utah and Colorado to Illinois, Texas and west into Arizona. They are also found in Mexico

CLASSIFICATION

ORDER SQUAMATA
SUBORDER SAURIA • 26 FAMILIES
420 GENERA • 4,300 SPECIES
FAMILY CROTAPHYTIDAE

A collared lizard devours a cricket.

Leopard Lizards

The two leopard lizard species live in flat areas with little vegetation, so they need to be fast runners. Some lizards use this vegetation for shelter. Others make use of small mammal burrows, such as abandoned ground squirrel tunnels and abandoned and occupied kangaroo rat tunnels, while some construct their own burrows. In the colder months the lizards hibernate in these burrows.

The leopard lizard Gambelia wislizenii is an agile lizard that often darts from bush to bush in search of its insect prey.

CLASSIFICATION

ORDER SQUAMATA
SUBORDER SAURIA • 26 FAMILIES
420 GENERA • 4,300 SPECIES
FAMILY CROTAPHYTIDAE

Characteristics Like their close relatives the collared lizards, these quick, active lizards have large heads and long limbs and tails. They range in total length from 9 to 15 inches (23–38 cm). As their common names suggest, the longnose leopard lizard has an elongated head while the endangered blunt-nosed leopard lizard has a blunt snout and a short, broad triangular head. The females of both species develop red or orange markings on their sides, head and under their tail just before they lay eggs.

Diet Leopard lizards eat spiders and insects such as grasshoppers, crickets and moths. Larger leopard lizards also prey on smaller lizards.

Reproduction The female lays a clutch of two to six eggs once, and occasionally twice, a year in the summer months.

Habitat The leopard lizards live in flat, arid areas with sparse vegetation and loose, sandy or gravelly soil. They are found in south-west USA and northern Mexico.

LAVA LIZARDS

Lava lizards are small, agile and fast-moving species of the genus *Tropidurus*. Although they are popularly associated with the Galapagos Islands, they are also found in South and Central America. Their large numbers and bright colors make them conspicuous on the Galapagos Islands where, as their common name suggests, they scamper over the dark lava formations and rocks in search of prey.

CLASSIFICATION

ORDER SQUAMATA
SUBORDER SAURIA • 26 FAMILIES
420 GENERA • 4,300 SPECIES
FAMILY TROPIDURIDAE

Characteristics Lava lizards are sexually dimorphic—size and color differences between the sexes are quite obvious. During the breeding season the females develop red throats. The lizards have slender bodies, and are shaped rather like a small iguana.

Diet Lava lizards feed on insects and other invertebrates such as sand hoppers and spiders.

Reproduction A clutch of eggs is laid in a nest chamber dug into sandy soil.

Habitat These lizards are found on the mainland of South and Central America and on the Galapagos Islands. They are preyed upon by cats and rats.

The population of lava lizards in the Galapagos Islands is threatened by introduced animals.

GETTING IN TOUCH

Some lizard species live in colonies, but many spend much of their lives as solitary individuals, coming together only during the breeding season. Lizards usually communicate to defend their territory or to mate. Some lizards communicate with one another through highly stereotyped behavior. Others rely on color, smell and, in a few cases, sound.

Marine iguanas are usually a grayish black but when they are ready to mate, the spiny crests and limbs of the males turn green and their bodies become rusty red.

Movement Iguanas and dragon lizards wave one leg in the air, bob their heads or move their bodies up and down to let other lizards know they are ready to mate or to warn invaders to leave their territory. Other lizards send similar messages by raising their crest, extending or curling their dewlap, or lashing their tail.

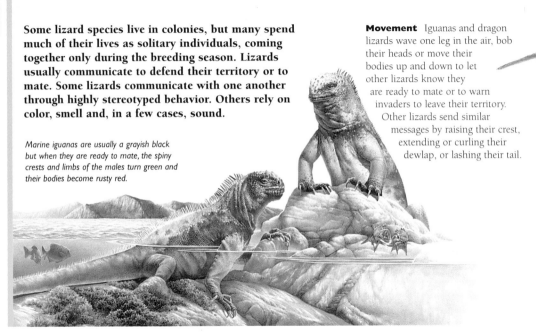

206

Color changes Some lizards use color to communicate. Male chameleons change color to threaten rivals, while other male lizards change color to let females know they are ready to mate. Some females change as well. Collared and leopard lizard females develop red or orange markings on their sides, head and under their tail just before they lay eggs. This may let males know they are not interested in mating.

The Knysna dwarf chameleon Bradypodion damaranum is predominantly green at rest but males develop the bright color pattern shown here as a threat display to other males.

Airborne messages
The fork-tongued lizards rely more on chemical cues for information. They recognize potential mates and rivals, as well as prey, from pheromones and other chemicals produced by these animals. The lizards flick out their tongue to collect molecules from the air or the ground, then carry them to the roof of the mouth where an organ called the Jacobson's organ recognizes them.

Collared lizards communicate with each other by bobbing their heads up and down. If a rival invades their territory, they do "push-ups" that make them look bigger.

Vocalization A few lizard groups are known to vocalize, with geckos having the most spectacular voices. It may be that the nocturnal geckos developed noises for communicating in the dark. They make chirping, clicking or barking sounds, and have different sounds for courting or defending a territory.

207

VELVET GECKOS

The Australian velvet geckos have tiny, even scales which give their skin a velvety texture, hence their common name. They are secretive, nocturnal creatures. During the day the arboreal species hide behind loose bark or in hollow tree trunks, while the rock-dwellers wedge themselves into crevices or hide under rock slabs or in caves.

CLASSIFICATION

ORDER SQUAMATA
SUBORDER SAURIA • 26 FAMILIES
420 GENERA • 4,300 SPECIES
FAMILY GEKKONIDAE

Characteristics These geckos have plump tails where fat is stored for times when food is scarce. As long as water is available they can survive without food for six months or more. Several species have flattened bodies that help them squeeze into small hiding places. On their toes they have climbing pads and retractable claws. They vary in total length from 3 to 6 inches (7–15 cm).

Diet Velvet geckos feed on insects, spiders and other arthropods. Some larger individuals prey on smaller lizards.

Reproduction Two eggs are usually laid in moist litter-filled rock crevices or under bark.

Habitat Some live under rock slabs or outcrops; others prefer tree hollows or under bark in Australian open forests and woodlands.

The southern spotted velvet gecko Oedura tryoni *is found on granite outcrops on the east coast of Australia.*

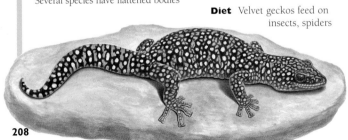

RING-TAILED GECKO

The ring-tailed gecko *Cyrtodactylus louisiadensis* is one of the largest geckos in Australia. Usually it forages for food on the ground or on rocks or cliff faces, but it is an excellent climber and can sometimes be seen perched on low branches or tree trunks. If disturbed it will quickly retreat to the safety of a hollow limb, rock crevice or cave.

CLASSIFICATION

ORDER SQUAMATA
SUBORDER SAURIA • 26 FAMILIES
420 GENERA • 4,300 SPECIES
FAMILY GEKKONIDAE

Characteristics The dark brown and white bands on this gecko's long, slender tail give it its common name. The gecko has reduced climbing pads, but its long, bent, almost bird-like claws make it an efficient climber. It grows to an average total length of about 10 inches (25 cm).

Diet The ring-tailed gecko preys on and eats large insects such as tree crickets and beetles, as well as small lizards

Reproduction It lays clutches of one to two eggs usually in a damp rock crevice or under the bark of a tree.

Habitat The ring-tailed gecko lives in woodlands, rocky outcrops and rainforest areas in the far north-east of Australia and in New Guinea.

209

LEOPARD GECKO

The leopard gecko *Eublepharis macularius* belongs
to a family of geckos that have moveable eyelids.
In most geckos, the eyelids have been replaced by
a fixed transparent scale that protects the eyes.
Another difference is that the feet of the geckos
in the family Eublepharidae do not have the adhesive
climbing pads typical of many other geckos.

CLASSIFICATION

ORDER SQUAMATA
SUBORDER SAURIA • 26 FAMILIES
420 GENERA • 4,300 SPECIES
FAMILY EUBLEPHARIDAE

Characteristics The leopard
gecko has a relatively short, fat tail
and short limbs. Its slightly flattened
body and small size help it to hide
in rock crevices and under dry
scrub. Its common name derives
from its multitude of black spots
and blotches on a yellow
background. Adults reach about
8 inches (20 cm) in length.

Diet The leopard gecko feeds
mostly on insects, including crickets,
and worms.

Reproduction The female lays
a clutch of two to four eggs which
hatch after about two months. The
sex of the young may be determined
by the temperature experienced by
the embryo in its egg.

Habitat More terrestrial than
most other geckos, the leopard gecko
is native to Iran, India, Afghanistan
and Pakistan.

BANDED GECKO

When hunting for food, the small banded gecko *Coleonyx variegatus* stalks its victim on straight, stiff legs, and then pounces when it is very close, capturing the prey in its jaws. After eating, the gecko cleans its face with its tongue. The nocturnal banded gecko is inactive for as much as half the year when night temperatures fall below about 73°F (23°C).

CLASSIFICATION

ORDER SQUAMATA
SUBORDER SAURIA • 26 FAMILIES
420 GENERA • 4,300 SPECIES
FAMILY EUBLEPHARIDAE

Characteristics The banded gecko has large eyes and moveable eyelids. It has pointed claws but no climbing pads on its slender toes. Its skin is thin and translucent, and it has a plump tail where fat is stored for times when food is scarce. When protecting its territory against other males or when captured, it emits a squeak or chirp.

Diet Banded geckos eat insects, spiders, baby scorpions and other small arthropods, often hunting for their prey in rodent burrows.

Reproduction Females lay clutches of two eggs one to three times during the warmer months.

Habitat The gecko occupies many habitats, avoiding the heat of the day under logs or debris or in moist rock crevices. It is found in the rocky and sandy desert and semi-desert areas of southwest USA and Mexico.

DAY GECKOS

Day geckos—species of the genus *Phelsuma*—are notable for their bright coloring. They are active during the day, when they can be seen scampering through the tropical forests and coconut plantations of Madagascar and their other island homes, or sheltering under rocky outcrops, well camouflaged by their cryptic coloring. The largest day geckos grow to about 10 inches (25 cm) in length.

Characteristics Day geckos have greatly reduced claws and rely entirely on their well-developed toe pads when climbing. Most species are a rich green, often patterned with red and blue spots; others, however, are quite plain with dark olive or gray-brown coloring.

Diet In addition to taking arthropod prey such as insects and spiders, day geckos have been

A day gecko from the island of Madagascar. Like all members of the genus Phelsuma, *it has round pupils and greatly reduced claws on its digits, relying solely on its toe pads when climbing.*

known to eat fruit, and the nectar and pollen from flowers.

Reproduction Courtship displays involve head bobbing and tail waving. The females lay one or two eggs, which are often attached to each other and secreted in a rocky hiding place. Unlike most lizards, which produce eggs with leathery shells, the day geckos (and all geckos of the family Gekkonidae) lay eggs with hard, brittle shells. Normally, only one clutch is laid per season,

although additional clutches may be laid if environmental conditions are favorable.

Habitat Day geckos are distributed in Madagascar and other islands—the Seychelles, Comoros, Andamans and smaller islands in the Indian Ocean off the coast of East Africa. An endemic species, the Namaqua day gecko, has a restricted range in western South Africa and southern Namibia.

CLASSIFICATION

ORDER SQUAMATA
SUBORDER SAURIA • 26 FAMILIES
420 GENERA • 4,300 SPECIES
FAMILY GEKKONIDAE

COLORFUL ISLANDER
The blue-tailed day gecko *Phelsuma cepediana* is a colorful gecko from the islands of Réunion and Mauritius. It is active during the daytime and a tree-dweller.

213

SPECIAL LIMBS AND TOES

Long and slender, short and stout—most lizards have four well-developed legs, but they come in many styles to suit their particular environment. Their toes, too, may have strong claws for climbing or digging, fringes for shimmying through sand, or even webbing for gliding or swimming.

Lizard locomotion To move forward, lizards usually move one front and the opposite hind leg at the same time. This produces their characteristic wriggling, or undulating, movement. Some species have very powerful hind legs, and when moving rapidly lift their front legs off the ground and run on the two back legs. This is known as bipedal locomotion.

DESERT DIVER
Aided by the fringes on its long toes, the Mohave fringe-toed lizard *Uma scoparia* escapes predators by diving into a sand dune and "swimming" to safety. Other adaptations that prevent sand getting into its nose, eyes, ears and mouth include the ability to close its nostrils, interlocking scales on its upper and lower eyelids, flaps over its ears, and an upper jaw that overlaps the lower one.

Sand shoes Many sand-dwelling lizards have webbed feet or fringed toes to help them grip shifting sand. The fringes (left), formed by a row of enlarged scales on the borders of the toes, enlarge the surface area of the feet. This helps the lizards bury themselves in the sand or, in the case of the sandfish of Asia and North Africa, move freely through loose sand, an action referred to as "sand swimming." The webbing on the desert gecko's foot (below right) helps it dig burrows and run across the sand dunes.

A stroll on the ceiling Many lizards climb but only a few have evolved adhesive toe pads that enable them to scale surfaces as smooth as glass. These toe pads occur in a few skink species and the anoles, but it is the geckos,

With its prehensile tail and the two pairs of opposing toes on each foot that provide a pincer-like grip, this Parsons chameleon Chamaeleo parsonii from Madagascar has no trouble climbing along slender twigs.

famous for their ability to run up smooth vertical surfaces and even walk upside-down on ceilings, that are the most accomplished of the lizard climbers.

Disappearing limbs Over thousands of years, some lizards have developed reduced limbs or lost their limbs altogether. These lizards usually burrow underground, or live in habitats where limbs would be of little use, such as areas with many narrow crevices or where the vegetation is low and dense.

A GREAT GRIP
At the end of a climbing gecko's toe are enlarged overlapping plates. On each plate are thousands of microscopic, hair-like projections that cling to invisible rough spots, allowing the gecko to walk up walls.

FLAP-FOOTED LIZARDS

With their extremely long bodies, tiny hindlimbs and no forelimbs, these lizards look remarkably like snakes. Though small, the lizards sometimes use their hindlimbs to move through vegetation and in courtship and defensive behaviors. Some species live underground, while others live on the surface, retreating to the burrows of spiders or other animals or into dense clumps of spinifex grass for shelter.

CLASSIFICATION

ORDER SQUAMATA
SUBORDER SAURIA • 26 FAMILIES
420 GENERA • 4,300 SPECIES
FAMILY PYGOPODIDAE

Characteristics The hindlimbs of these lizards are small, flattened flaps that normally lie flat against the sides of the body. They have a transparent scale over their eyes which they wipe clean with their tongue. Many species have an extremely long tail that can be discarded if the lizard is attacked.

The largest, most common flap-footed lizard, Burton's snake-lizard *Lialis burtonis*, is 23 inches (59 cm) long.

Diet Most species eat insects and other arthropods. Burton's snake-lizard eats other lizards, mainly skinks, and snakes.

Reproduction All flap-footed lizards lay clutches of two eggs.

Habitat Most prefer semi-arid and arid habitats with low, dense vegetation. They occur in Australia with two species in New Guinea.

When agitated, the flap-footed lizard Delma tincta uses the strong muscles in its long tail to lift its entire body off the ground. It may jump several times, changing direction with each jump.

GLASS LIZARDS

These ground-dwelling lizards are completely legless. Their tails are extremely long—sometimes twice the length of their body—and their common name comes from their tendency to readily discard the tail when threatened. Most species are secretive animals, hiding under logs, vegetation or in burrows. During winter, glass lizards hibernate in the deep tunnels made by other animals such as rodents and moles.

CLASSIFICATION

ORDER SQUAMATA
SUBORDER SAURIA • 26 FAMILIES
420 GENERA • 4,300 SPECIES
FAMILY ANGUIDAE

Characteristics There is a wide variety of species of legless lizards, with stiff bodies, closeable eyelids and fragile tails.

Diet The sheltopusik feeds on small mammals, snails, insects and other reptiles. The smaller species usually eat insects but they may take young mammals from nests, small amphibians and reptiles too.

Reproduction All glass lizards lay eggs and in some species, the female stays with the eggs during incubation, though she does not actively defend the nest.

Habitat Glass lizards occur in a range of habitats from stony steppes to tallgrass prairies and damp forests. They are found in North America, southern Europe, south-western Asia and North Africa.

Reaching total lengths of up to 4½ ft (1.4 m), the sheltopusik Ophisaurus apodus of Europe and Asia is the largest glass lizard. Less secretive than other species, it can often be seen basking on the branches of low bushes.

THE NEXT GENERATION

Most lizards lay eggs but some species give birth to live young. A few lizards guard their eggs against predators, but most simply bury them in soil or leaves and abandon them. Lizards are able to look after themselves as soon as they hatch, but they have many predators and very few young lizards survive to breed.

The Australian blue-tongued skink gives birth to several live young.

Eggs and nests Some geckos and skinks lay only one or two eggs while larger lizards lay 40 or more with a clutch of around 20 being common. Lizards may dig holes for nests and cover them over or they make use of ready-made hiding places such as a rotting log. The eggs usually take from two weeks to three months to hatch depending on the temperature of the nest, though some take much longer. The eggs of most lizards have a leathery shell, but some geckos lay hard-shelled eggs that often stick to tree bark or leaves. If the eggs are on a branch that is broken off in a storm and washed out to sea, currents may carry the log and the eggs to another island. Geckos occur on many islands that other lizards have not reached.

Live young Some lizards produce live young. In most cases the embryos are in eggs inside the mother's body, with the developing young being nourished by the yolk in the same way as young that grow in eggs outside the body. In a few lizards, such as the night lizards and some skinks, a placenta forms so the young obtain nourishment directly from the mother.

HOUSE GUESTS
Some species of goannas (Australian monitors) keep their eggs warm and safe by laying them in termite mounds. When the eggs are ready to hatch, the female scrapes away the hard soil of the mound to let the young escape.

Parental care Most lizards abandon their eggs once they are laid, but a few species do guard them against predators. Some North American skinks, for example, coil their body around the eggs until they hatch. Some lizards clean and rotate the eggs and a few of the live-bearing species, such as the desert night lizard, seem to assist the young from the fetal membrane.

Single parents
Some chameleons, dragon lizards, night lizards, whiptail lizards, wall lizards and geckos reproduce without males. The eggs of these lizards do not need to be fertilized by males to develop. These all-female lizards increase in number faster than those that have male and female parents.

The Nullarbor bearded dragon lays its eggs in a nest scraped out of sand in the Australian desert.

ALLIGATOR LIZARDS

These slow-moving lizards have large, rough squarish scales that give them their common name. Their dark brown mottled skin, which they shed in one piece like a snake, increases this likeness to alligators. Many species live in the trees in the rainforests of Central and South America. The ground dwellers are generally secretive creatures that hide in the undergrowth, in rocky crevices or down burrows.

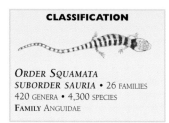

CLASSIFICATION

ORDER SQUAMATA
SUBORDER SAURIA • 26 FAMILIES
420 GENERA • 4,300 SPECIES
FAMILY ANGUIDAE

Characteristics Alligator lizards have a flat, wedge-shaped head. They are slender with small, thin limbs and a long tail which in some species is prehensile. They grow to about 12 inches (30 cm) in length.

Diet Diet varies according to size. They eat insects, scorpions, spiders, snails, millipedes, birds, small mammals and other lizards.

The southern alligator lizard Elgaria multicarinata *from North America is a ground dweller but it also climbs trees with the aid of its partly prehensile tail.*

Reproduction Most species lay eggs in burrows or other protected sites. However, the northern alligator lizard *Elgaria coerulea*, which is adapted to colder conditions, gives birth to live young three months after mating.

Habitat Alligator lizards occupy a wide range of habitats from deserts and tropical lowlands to heavily forested mountains. Their distribution ranges from southwestern Canada to tropical Central and South America.

BEADED LIZARDS

The two beaded lizards, the gila monster and the Mexican beaded lizard, are the only venomous lizards. The venom is used for defense as these slow-moving lizards spend long periods exposed in open habitats while foraging for food. Beaded lizards avoid high temperatures, spending much of their time in burrows. Only in the cooler spring months or when the weather is overcast are they active during the day.

CLASSIFICATION

ORDER SQUAMATA
SUBORDER SAURIA • 26 FAMILIES
420 GENERA • 4,300 SPECIES
FAMILY HELODERMATIDAE

Characteristics These are large lizards—the gila monster reaches a total length of 2 feet (60 cm) and the Mexican beaded lizard 3 feet (1 m). They are stocky with broad heads and short tails used for fat storage. Their scales are small and bead-like and do not overlap.

Diet Both species feed on a variety of prey but rely heavily on the nest young of rodents and other small mammals, and bird and reptile eggs. They forage on the ground but may climb low trees in search of prey.

Reproduction Intense combat between rival males usually precedes mating. The eggs are laid in sandy soil, under rocks or in a burrow. The young hatch about 10 months later.

Habitat Gila monsters are usually found on rocky slopes in areas of desert scrub, grassland or oak woods. They occur in south-western USA and north-western Mexico. Mexican beaded lizards inhabit desert scrub and tropical woodlands. They occur along the west coast of Mexico and Guatemala.

A gila monster Heloderma suspectum *swallows a mouse.*

221

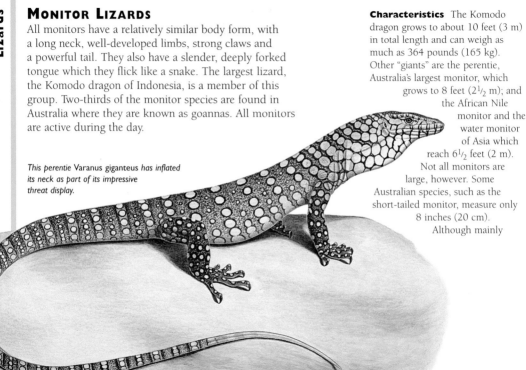

MONITOR LIZARDS

All monitors have a relatively similar body form, with a long neck, well-developed limbs, strong claws and a powerful tail. They also have a slender, deeply forked tongue which they flick like a snake. The largest lizard, the Komodo dragon of Indonesia, is a member of this group. Two-thirds of the monitor species are found in Australia where they are known as goannas. All monitors are active during the day.

This perentie Varanus giganteus *has inflated its neck as part of its impressive threat display.*

Characteristics The Komodo dragon grows to about 10 feet (3 m) in total length and can weigh as much as 364 pounds (165 kg). Other "giants" are the perentie, Australia's largest monitor, which grows to 8 feet (2½ m); and the African Nile monitor and the water monitor of Asia which reach 6½ feet (2 m). Not all monitors are large, however. Some Australian species, such as the short-tailed monitor, measure only 8 inches (20 cm). Although mainly terrestrial, many monitors are proficient tree climbers. The emerald tree monitor of New Guinea and northern Australia is an arboreal specialist with a long prehensile tail. Aquatic species, like Merten's water monitor, have a flattened, paddle-like tail which is used for swimming.

Diet The prey of monitor lizards relates to their size. They are mostly insectivorous, especially the smaller ones. The medium-sized species eat insects, small lizards and small mammals. The arboreal species will take young birds from nests and the aquatic ones include fish and frogs in their diet. Large monitors eat small mammals, birds, other lizards and carrion. The largest Komodo dragons will bring down wild pigs, deer and even water buffalo. Many monitors have a liking for eggs. The Asian water monitor digs up turtle eggs and the Nile monitor searches for crocodile nests to raid.

GOANNA ON GUARD
Gould's monitor *Varanus gouldii*, Australia's most widespread monitor, uses its tail as a prop to stand up and survey its surroundings. It will also rear up like this when threatened by a rival or an enemy, though in the latter case it is more likely to dash to the nearest burrow.

CLASSIFICATION

ORDER SQUAMATA
SUBORDER SAURIA • 26 FAMILIES
420 GENERA • 4,300 SPECIES
FAMILY VARANIDAE

Reproduction Male monitors compete for the females. They rise up on their hind legs and the base of their tail, and "wrestle." The victor is the one who pushes his opponent over. After mating, the females lay seven to 37 eggs, usually in the soil or in tree stumps or hollows.

Habitat Monitors live in rocky and sandy deserts, rainforests, open woodlands and forests, and along river banks and in mangroves They are found in Australia, South-East Asia and Africa.

GIRDLE-TAILED LIZARDS

These heavily armored lizards have large, rectangular scales arranged in regular rows around their body. On the back of their head and on their tail are rings, or "girdles," of sharp spines. These lizards use their tail as a weapon to defend themselves, or to plug up a burrow or wedge themselves into a rocky crevice. Active during the day, girdle-tails are all sun-loving, basking lizards.

CLASSIFICATION

ORDER SQUAMATA
SUBORDER SAURIA • 26 FAMILIES
420 GENERA • 4,300 SPECIES
FAMILY CORDYLIDAE

Characteristics The body and head of these lizards are flattened. The largest is the sungazer which reaches nearly 16 inches (40 cm) in total length. Most species are drab, with browns, blacks and straw colors dominating.

Diet The lizards feed mainly on insects but some of the larger species also eat plant matter such as fallen fruit, berries and lichen.

Reproduction All the girdle-tailed lizards produce live young, usually with one to six young in each litter.

Habitat Girdle-tailed lizards are mainly rock dwellers and live in semi-arid to arid areas. The lizards occur in Africa and are particularly numerous in southern Africa.

A PRICKLY BALL

When threatened in the open, the armadillo girdle-tailed lizard *Cordylus cataphractus* rolls itself into a ball and clamps its tail in its mouth, thus shielding its soft and vulnerable underside. Groups of related individuals often live together in deep rock cracks in the arid zone of South Africa.

FLAT LIZARDS

These lizards have an amazingly flat head and body which allows them to squeeze into the narrowest of rock crevices. Often large numbers of individuals will be found sheltering together in a thin space beneath a rock flake. In many species the males become vibrantly colored during the breeding season. A common color combination is bright green on top, an orange tail, and electric blue underneath.

CLASSIFICATION

ORDER SQUAMATA
SUBORDER SAURIA • 26 FAMILIES
420 GENERA • 4,300 SPECIES
FAMILY CORDYLIDAE

Characteristics The flat lizards grow to a total length of about 12 inches (30 cm) but they are less than half an inch (1 cm) thick. The females and juveniles do not develop the bright colors of the males but they have a striped back.

Diet Insects make up the main part of the lizards' diet, but occasionally they eat plant matter.

Reproduction Flat lizards are the only members of the family Cordylidae to lay eggs. Two or so eggs are laid in a deep, damp crack in the rock, and a single site may be shared by 10 or more females.

Habitat Flat lizards live on rocky outcrops or boulders in the arid regions of south-eastern Africa.

A male dwarf flat lizard Platysaurus guttatus *in his breeding colors.*

WALL LIZARDS

These lizards are very familiar to most Europeans. Although they prefer open country, they can often be seen climbing on trees or rocks, or basking on old stone walls. Most species are terrestrial and are active during the day. They prefer high body temperatures so become inactive when weather conditions are unfavorable, and many species spend the winter hibernating among stones or rocks or underground.

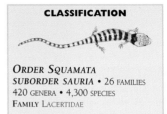

CLASSIFICATION

ORDER SQUAMATA
SUBORDER SAURIA • 26 FAMILIES
420 GENERA • 4,300 SPECIES
FAMILY LACERTIDAE

Characteristics These lizards have a long body with a pointed head, well-developed limbs and a long tapering tail that can be easily shed. They grow to a total length of around 5 1/2 inches (14 cm).

The males are often brightly colored, with green being the most common color, but the females and juveniles are more brown or gray.

Diet Wall lizards eat mainly insects, their larvae and other small invertebrates, but some species also eat succulent plants and soft fruit.

Reproduction Wall lizards lay small clutches of between three and six eggs in a hole dug in the soil. Those from the warmer regions lay several clutches a year.

Habitat These lizards make use of many habitats, such as rocks, the spaces between walls and old buildings. They are found in the arid regions of central and southern Europe and on the Channel Islands.

The color of the Italian wall lizard Podarcis sicula *changes according to which Mediterranean island it lives on.*

VIVIPAROUS LIZARD

As its name suggests, the viviparous lizard *Lacerta vivipara* gives birth to live young. It retains the eggs in its body until they hatch. This feature allows the lizard to succeed in harsh climates that could not be colonized by egg-laying species. By retaining the developing embryos within the body, the female can regulate the temperature and moisture more closely than if the eggs were left to develop outside the body.

Characteristics This small, agile lizard has a slender body and strong limbs, and grows to about 5 inches (13 cm), half of which is its long, tapering tail. The females are slightly longer and stockier than the males.

Diet Viviparous lizards eat whatever insect happens to be available, as well as spiders, centipedes, slugs and snails.

Reproduction The litter size of the viviparous lizards is generally four to eleven. The young are born in early summer, giving them time to feed before the winter hibernation.

Habitat These terrestrial lizards live in a wide range of habitats including meadows, moors, woodlands, gardens, mountains and sand dunes. They are widespread and occur in northern Asia and throughout Europe, extending into the Arctic Circle in Scandinavia.

WHIPTAIL LIZARDS

These slender, agile lizards have a high optimum body temperature. As a result they burn up lots of energy and need plenty of food. They are active foragers, at times moving almost constantly in search of prey. When threatened they can run incredibly fast, thus giving rise to their other common name, racerunners. During the cooler parts of the day and throughout the winter, the lizards retreat to burrows.

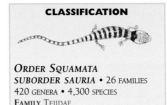

CLASSIFICATION

ORDER SQUAMATA
SUBORDER SAURIA • 26 FAMILIES
420 GENERA • 4,300 SPECIES
FAMILY TEIIDAE

Characteristics Whiptails are usually brown in color, though some of the tropical species are bright blue or green, and most have some sort of striped pattern. They have large scales on their head and tiny ones on their back, well-developed limbs, and a long tapering tail.

Diet Insects and other arthropods are the main part of the whiptails' diet. Prey such as termites are often excavated by digging.

Reproduction Small clutches of one to six eggs are usual, with some species laying twice a year. Several whiptail species are all-female and are able to produce fertile eggs without mating with males.

Habitat The terrestrial whiptails occupy a variety of habitats, from deserts to tropical forests. They occur from southern USA to Argentina and in the West Indies.

The checkered whiptail Cnemidophorus tesselatus of North America is an all-female species.

JUNGLE RUNNERS

The jungle runners of tropical Central and South America are efficient predators. As well as snapping up insects with their powerful jaws, they also prey on birds, small mammals and other reptiles. In behavior and form the jungle runners resemble the smaller European lizards. The common jungle runner *Ameiva ameiva* is also known as the Surinam lizard; a related species is the South American striped lizard *Ameiva undulatus*.

Characteristics These lizards are essentially larger versions of the whiptails, growing to a total length of up to 20 inches (50 cm). They are usually brown in color though in some species the males have bright markings on the back and sides. Their tails are long and their tongues deeply cleft.

Diet Jungle runners eat spiders and insects like beetles, cockroaches and caterpillars, as well as small birds, mammals and reptiles. They also eat small amounts of leaves and fruit.

Reproduction Females lay small clutches of two to six eggs which they bury in sand or loose soil.

Habitat Jungle runners occupy a wide range of habitats but they are often seen along river banks or in forest clearings. They are found in tropical Central and South America.

The common jungle runner Ameiva ameiva *is widespread throughout much of Latin America.*

NIGHT LIZARDS

These small lizards have a low preferred body temperature. They are most active at 73°F (23°C) which is 10 degrees lower than most lizards. A few species are active by day, usually in dark, cool hidden places, but most are nocturnal or active at twilight. Night lizards occupy rotting logs, caves or cracks and crevices in rocks, while others hide under dead leaves or low-lying bushes.

CLASSIFICATION

ORDER SQUAMATA
SUBORDER SAURIA • 26 FAMILIES
420 GENERA • 4,300 SPECIES
FAMILY XANTUSIIDAE

Characteristics Like geckos, these lizards have a transparent scale which protects their eyes, rather than an eyelid. In color, most are inconspicuous grays or browns, the exception being the granite night lizard which has distinctive markings.

Diet Most night lizards eat insects, but a few species include plant matter such as figs, fruit or seeds in their diet.

Reproduction All species give birth to between one and eight live young after a gestation period of three months..

Habitat Night lizards live in tropical lowland forests and in rocky semi-arid zones. They are found in south-western USA, Central America and the West Indies.

The somewhat flattened body of the granite night lizard Xantusia henshawi *allows it to slide easily in and out of rock crevices.*

NAMIB DUNE LIZARD

The African Namib dune lizard *Aporosaura anchietae* is a specialized desert dweller. Although it can withstand high temperatures, to reduce the transfer of heat from the sand, it does a "thermal dance," alternately lifting two feet while balancing on the other two. To escape the intense heat of the midday sun, it buries itself in the sand. The body is sand-colored with a network of black markings.

CLASSIFICATION

ORDER SQUAMATA
SUBORDER SAURIA • 26 FAMILIES
420 GENERA • 4,300 SPECIES
FAMILY LACERTIDAE

Characteristics This lizard's alternative common name, shovel-snouted lizard, points to one of the ways it has adapted to living in the desert. When disturbed or pursued, it dives into the dune face, using its flattened snout—which has a sharp cutting edge—and powerful hind legs to "swim" deep into the sand. If it cannot escape, it will raise its body, jump and bite. These lizards are territorial, particularly during the breeding season, and males will defend choice territories such as areas where seeds collect.

Diet This lizard eats small beetles and other insects but will also eat windblown seeds when insects are not available.

Reproduction One or two large eggs are laid in a chamber dug into firm sand in a dune. There is no fixed breeding season.

Habitat This lizard is endemic to the Namib Desert on the west coast of southern Africa. Its preferred habitat is sparsely vegetated desert sand dunes.

PINK-TONGUED SKINK

There are more than 1,300 species of skinks, making this the largest of the lizard families. Although it can climb small shrubs and trees, the Australian pink-tongued skink usually forages for its prey among ground litter and low vegetation. When threatened, it faces its attacker and stands its ground, hissing and flicking its bright pink tongue. It shelters under loose tree bark or rock shelves, or in cracks and crevices.

CLASSIFICATION

ORDER SQUAMATA
SUBORDER SAURIA • 26 FAMILIES
420 GENERA • 4,300 SPECIES
FAMILY SCINCIDAE

Though the pink-tongued skink
Cyclodomorphus gerrardii *can be active by day in cooler areas, it is usually nocturnal.*

Characteristics This skink grows to an overall length of around 17 inches (45 cm), about half of which is its prehensile tail. This, along with its strong claws, is useful for climbing. Like most skinks, it has smooth, overlapping scales. The newborn lizards have blue rather than pink tongues.

Diet The pink-tongued skink eats some insects, but its diet is made up mainly of slugs and snails.

Reproduction Like many skinks, the pink-tongued skink gives birth to live young. The litter is usually large, from 12 to 25 young, but the newborn lizards are very small.

Habitat The pink-tongued skink lives in rainforests and other wet forest areas along the coast of eastern Australia from mid New South Wales to the northern tip of Queensland.

EMERALD TREE SKINK

This Asian–Pacific skink *Lamprolepis smaragdina* has a long tail, slightly depressed head and slender snout. Its well-developed limbs assist as it climbs and scuttles along tree trunks. It grows to 4 inches (10 cm) in head–body length, although the tail is equally as long, and can be longer. Its mottled green color ensures that it is well camouflaged in its tropical forest habitat.

CLASSIFICATION

ORDER SQUAMATA
SUBORDER SAURIA • 26 FAMILIES
420 GENERA • 4,300 SPECIES
FAMILY SCINCIDAE

Characteristics The green emerald tree skink is aptly named. Its underside ranges from yellow to greenish white. It is active during the day and is a tree dweller, although it occasionally descends to the ground in search of food. It is swift in movement and very agile as it darts along tree trunks and branches.

Diet The emerald tree skink is mainly an insect eater, but it will also eat fruit and flowers if insects are not available.

Reproduction This is an egg-laying species, laying its two eggs in humus or rotting timber on or above the ground.

Habitat This skink is widely distributed in Asia and the Pacific, from Taiwan and the Philippines through several Pacific islands to Indonesia, New Guinea and the Solomons. It prefers larger forest trees and has adapted to human settlement—it is common in the palms of coconut plantations in some areas.

RED-TAILED SKINK

The small, sun-loving red-tailed skink *Morethia ruficauda* is often most active at midday when temperatures in the north of Australia where it lives are high. A terrestrial lizard, it forages among leaf litter and rocks for its food. It is swift and agile, quickly diving under the leaf litter if disturbed. If it is not fast enough, it can discard its bright red tail.

CLASSIFICATION

ORDER SQUAMATA
SUBORDER SAURIA • 26 FAMILIES
420 GENERA • 4,300 SPECIES
FAMILY SCINCIDAE

Characteristics The red-tailed skink has smooth, shiny scales, well-developed limbs, and a long, whip-like fragile tail. Individuals—presumably males—have been observed facing one another from a distance of 4 inches (10 cm) and whipping their tails horizontally, probably as an assertion of sexual or territorial rights. There are two subspecies, distinguished by variations in their color and body markings.

Diet The red-tailed skink eats arthropods and other small invertebrates, for which it forages among rocks and leaf litter.

Reproduction Mating occurs in spring and small clutches of eggs are laid in safe hiding places.

Habitat The red-tailed skink is widely distributed in arid and semi-arid rocky areas in north-western and central Australia. Its favored habitats are the margins of rock outcrops and stony soils.

FIVE-LINED SKINK

The juveniles of the widespread North American five-lined skink *Eumeces fasciatus* have black bodies with white stripes and bright blue tails, making them look remarkably similar to the unrelated Australian red-tailed skink. Tail loss is common and in many populations most of the adults have grown a new one. These skinks are terrestrial and will climb the lower reaches of trees only to bask.

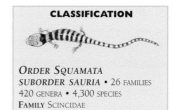

CLASSIFICATION

ORDER SQUAMATA
SUBORDER SAURIA • 26 FAMILIES
420 GENERA • 4,300 SPECIES
FAMILY SCINCIDAE

Characteristics The coloring of these skinks changes as they grow. The bright blue disappears, their bodies become brown, and the males lose the striped pattern as well. In the breeding season, increased levels of testosterone in the blood cause the males to develop bright orange heads. The skinks grow to a length of 5–8 inches (13–20 cm).

Diet The skink forages for insects, insect larvae, crustaceans, spiders, earthworms, other lizards and even small mice.

Reproduction The skinks mate in April or May. Clutches of four to 15 eggs are laid in decaying logs or under rocks. The eggs are guarded by the mother until they hatch in summer.

Habitat The five-lined skink is widely distributed in North America, from New England south to Florida, west to Texas and north to Kansas and Ontario. It prefers damp, wooded areas. decaying leaf litter, rotting stumps and logs but can also be seen in gardens.

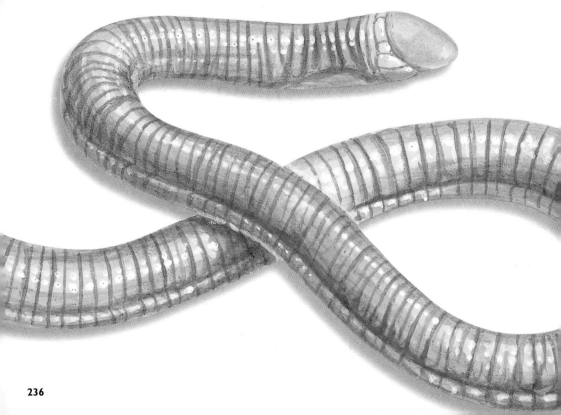

AMPHISBAENIANS

It was once thought that Amphisbaenians were lizards, but they are so well adapted for their life underground and so very different from lizards today that most scientists now consider they are an independent offshoot of the order Squamata. Thus the 140 species of amphisbaenians, or worm lizards, are placed in a separate suborder. There are four families of amphisbaenians and three of these have no legs at all. The fourth family, the Mexican worm lizards, have two strong front legs that are flattened like paddles. The legs help them move above ground and are used to sweep soil past their head when they are digging a tunnel.

AMPHISBAENIANS

Worm lizards spend most of their lives underground where they use their hard, strong heads to burrow through the soil. They may emerge at night to feed on the surface, but they are usually only seen if heavy rain floods their burrows. Worm lizards have no external ear openings, but they can sense vibrations in the ground. If they detect an insect crawling through the soil, they can dig very quickly and catch it.

Scales arranged like tiles stop the dirt from building up on the body of the shovel-snouted worm lizard.

Characteristics The skin of a worm lizard is loosely attached to its cylindrical body and is ringed with small scales. Special scales on the face allow it to detect sound vibrations. It has simplified eyes that can barely see movement, and can distinguish only between light and dark. On its snout is a large, reinforced scale which helps it force its way through the soil. The worm lizard's mouth is deeply recessed under the snout so dirt cannot get in when it is burrowing. The tail, pointed in some species, rounded in others, is covered in horny

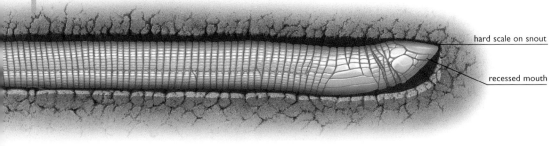

hard scale on snout

recessed mouth

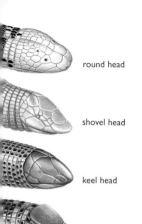

round head

shovel head

keel head

chisel head

DIFFERENT HEADS

The way worm lizards burrow is reflected in the shape of their head. Round-headed species push forward into the earth and turn the head in any direction to make the tunnel. Keel-headed species push the head forward and then to the side. Shovel-headed species push forward and then up. Chisel-headed species rotate the head in one direction and then the other.

scales to provide protection from predators. If grasped by a predator, it can be shed but a new one does not grow back. Worm lizards range in length from 4 to 30 inches (10–75 cm), with most being around 6–14 inches (15–35 cm).

Diet Amphisbaenians eat mostly insects, earthworms and other invertebrates. The larger species also eat small vertebrate animals and carrion. Worm lizards have sharp, interlocking teeth and powerful jaws so they can cut and tear pieces from larger prey.

Reproduction Most species lay eggs, but at least three species are known to retain the eggs inside their body and give birth to live young. Some species lay their eggs in ant or termite nests.

Habitat Amphisbaenians live in moist and sandy soil beneath the leaf litter in forests. They are

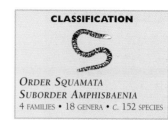
found in the warmer parts of Africa, the Middle East, southern Europe, South-East Asia, and Central and South America.

Keel-snouted worm lizards use their wedge-shaped snouts to scrape soil from the front of the tunnel, compressing it into the sides as they move forward.

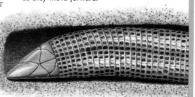

SNAKES

Many reptiles show evolutionary tendencies toward lengthening the body and reducing the limbs, but it is the snakes that have developed most successfully in this way. They have diversified dramatically during recent geological history and now inhabit most parts of the planet outside the polar regions. They come in a huge range of sizes, from the tiny thread snakes that are no bigger than a pencil to the giant anaconda, and their diets are equally diverse. Some feed on tiny eggs and the larvae of ants while others eat animals as large as antelopes and wallabies.

PIPE SNAKES

The pipe snakes are a small group of burrowing snakes that use their head to force their way through the damp soil and mud of the rice fields and swamps they inhabit. Although the Asian pipe snakes are usually quite dull in color, some species have brightly patterned undersides, especially the tail. If threatened, these snakes hide their head and wave their tail to distract the predator.

Characteristics The bones in the skull of the burrowing pipe snakes are solidly united, unlike those of most other snakes. Another unusual feature of the group is the presence of rudimentary hind legs in the form of small spurs on either side of the vent. The only South American pipe snake, the coral pipe snake, is a red and black banded snake with a blunt snout. It has small eyes covered by a transparent scale. The Asian pipe snakes are not as brightly colored. Most are dark brown with few, if any, markings on their back. The pipe snakes reach lengths of around 3 feet (1 m).

The blotched pipe snake Cylindrophus maculatus *from Sri Lanka raises its brightly colored tail in mimicry of a cobra's head and hood.*

Diet The coral pipe snake eats small mammals such as mice, caecilians, amphisbaenians, and small lizards and snakes. The Asian pipe snakes feed on eels and other snakes, sometimes catching and eating prey that exceeds their own body length.

Reproduction The coral pipe snake gives birth to between four and 10 live young. The Asian pipe snakes include both egg-laying and live-bearing species.

Habitat The South American coral pipe snake lives in swampy and marshy areas in the forests of the Amazon Basin. The Asian pipe snakes occur in lowland marshy areas and paddy fields. They are found in eastern Asia from Sri Lanka to Indonesia. The smallest of the group, the elegantly marked blotched pipe snake, inhabits forested (and formerly forested) areas of Sri Lanka.

"CORAL FALSA"
The close resemblance of the brightly patterned coral pipe snake *Anilius scytale* to the venomous coral snakes has resulted in its South American common name "coral falsa." Completely non-venomous, its main defense tactic is to hide its head and present its blunt tail as an alternative "head."

CLASSIFICATION

ORDER SQUAMATA • *SUBORDER SERPENTES* • *C.* 18 FAMILIES
C. 2,700 SPECIES • *C.* 450 GENERA
FAMILIES CYLINDROPHIDAE, ANILIIDAE

GREEN TREE PYTHON

The green tree python *Chondropython viridis* is a tree-dwelling snake whose brilliant green coloration camouflages it among the ferns and other epiphytic plants of its rainforest habitat. The snake hunts by night, sometimes coming down to the ground to search for its prey. The day is spent basking, draped in coils over a branch or vine. Sometimes it shelters in a tree hollow or among the large leaves of a fern.

CLASSIFICATION

ORDER SQUAMATA • SUBORDER SERPENTES • C. 18 FAMILIES C. 2,700 SPECIES • C. 450 GENERA FAMILY BOIDAE

Characteristics This solidly built tree-dweller can grow to an impressive 6½ feet (2 m) but it is more commonly about half this length. It has a large, broad head, which is distinct from the neck. An adept climber, it has a prehensile tail that it uses to grasp branches and to suspend itself from a height. The adult python is emerald green with a yellow belly and a stripe of white scales down its back. A nocturnal snake, it has large eyes with long vertical pupils that open up in the dark, and pale irises.

Diet Birds make up the main part of this snake's diet but it eats small mammals like rats and mice as well. The young also eat tree frogs. The python sometimes lures prey by wriggling the thin tip of its tail. When the prey comes to investigate, the python seizes it. It has been reported that the snake drinks rain water collected in its coils.

Reproduction The green tree python lays between 10 and 25 eggs in a clutch. When they first hatch green tree pythons are either bright yellow or a rich brick red. They stay this way for two or three years. Then, in a period of a few weeks, they change to the adult coloration. The skin is not shed at this time. Rather, in the center of each scale, a green speck appears that expands until the snake is green all over.

Habitat The green tree python inhabits tropical rainforests, monsoon forests and bamboo thickets. It is found in Papua New Guinea and in the far northern tip of eastern Australia.

A REMARKABLE CHANGE
Few pythons show such a marked change in body color between young and adult as that of the green tree python.

CARPET PYTHON

There are many pythons in
Australia, but the most widespread and familiar species is the
carpet python *Morelia spilota*. A good climber, it can be found
on tree branches and in hollows of trees, but it also shelters
in animal burrows, caves, rock crevices and below boulders.
It is mainly nocturnal though sometimes basks and forages
for food during the day.

Reproduction The female lays her
eggs in a sheltered place like a tree
hollow or abandoned burrow then
coils her body around them until
they hatch. Sometimes she will leave
the eggs to bask, returning when she
has raised her body temperature.

Characteristics Carpet pythons
come in many colors and patterns.
The attractive black and yellow
specimen above is from tropical
north-east Queensland. They
generally grow to 6½ feet (2 m) but
some are nearly twice this length.

Diet Carpet pythons feed on birds
and mammals and sometimes lizards.
Like all pythons, they throw a series
of coils around their prey as soon as
it is caught and suffocate it by
tightening the coils each time
the trapped animal exhales.

Habitat The carpet python
occupies almost all possible habitats
wherever it occurs, from wet tropical
rainforests to semi-arid deserts. It
is found over much of southern,
eastern and northern Australia and
also occurs in New Guinea.

BLOOD PYTHON

The blood python *Python curtus* is a short, semi-aquatic snake from South-East Asia where it inhabits swamps, marshes and slow-moving rainforest streams. Its common name is derived from the deep red coloring of some individuals. Because of its thick and stumpy tail, the blood python is also known as the short-tailed python.

Characteristics This stumpy species grows to almost 10 feet (3 m) in length. In color, its broad head ranges from red to yellowish or even gray, and the snake's overall body color is similarly variable, ranging from yellow to brick red with yellowish or brown blotches.

Diet The blood python feeds almost wholly on birds and small mammals. It is a nocturnal predator, lying in wait for prey partially submerged in ditches, pools or on the banks of rivers.

Reproduction The female lays from 10 to 15 eggs and coils around them to protect them until they hatch three months later.

Habitat This snake inhabits swamps or rainforest through southern Indo-China, Malaya, Sumatra and Borneo.

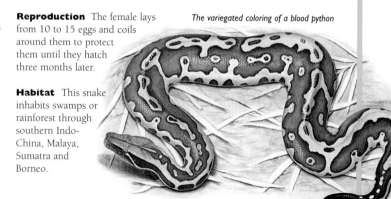

The variegated coloring of a blood python

247

WOMA PYTHON

The ground-dwelling woma python *Aspidites ramsayi* catches much of its prey in burrows where there is not enough room to throw its coils around it. Instead the woma pushes a loop of its body against the unlucky animal so it is squeezed against the side of the burrow. Many adult womas are covered in scars from retaliating rodents, as this technique doesn't immobilize prey as quickly as "normal" constriction.

CLASSIFICATION

ORDER SQUAMATA • SUBORDER SERPENTES • C. 18 FAMILIES C. 2,700 SPECIES • C. 450 GENERA **FAMILY BOIDAE**

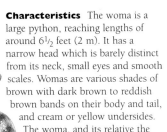

Characteristics The woma is a large python, reaching lengths of around 6½ feet (2 m). It has a narrow head which is barely distinct from its neck, small eyes and smooth scales. Womas are various shades of brown with dark brown to reddish brown bands on their body and tail, and cream or yellow undersides. The woma, and its relative the black-headed python, are the only pythons without the heat-sensitive pits in the upper lip that are used by other pythons to help locate warm-blooded prey.

Diet The woma eats birds, mammals such as hopping mice and small carnivorous marsupials, and reptiles, including venomous snakes.

Reproduction .Between six and 10 eggs are laid in burrows or crevices.

Habitat A generally nocturnal snake, the woma shelters during the day in hollow logs and abandoned burrows, mainly those of monitor lizards and mammals. It lives in rocky and sandy habitats in the desert regions of central Australia.

RETICULATED PYTHON

The record for the "longest snake in the world" belongs either to the reticulated python *Python reticulatus* of Asia, or to the South American anaconda. Both have been measured at around 33 feet (10 m), but the anaconda is a much heavier, thicker-bodied snake than the more slender reticulated python.

CLASSIFICATION

ORDER SQUAMATA • SUBORDER
SERPENTES • C. 18 FAMILIES
C. 2,700 SPECIES • C. 450 GENERA
FAMILY BOIDAE

Characteristics Like many nocturnal snakes, the reticulated python has narrow, vertical pupils. Its color varies from purplish brown to tan, with a chain of darker markings. The head is yellowish, with a darker line. This python is largely a tree-dweller but sometimes descends to the ground in search of food. It kills its prey by constriction.

Diet The reticulated python has been known to attack and feed on mammals and domestic fowl.

Reproduction Reticulated pythons usually lay large clutches of around 50 eggs, but clutches of up to 100 have been recorded. When the young hatch they are already around 2 feet (60 cm) long.

Habitat This massive python lives in the forests of South-East Asia, India, Bangladesh, Indo-China and the Philippines.

The reticulated python is one of the world's longest snakes.

NEW LIFE

Each spring in mild climates and just before the rainy season in the tropics, snakes begin to mate and reproduce. Most snakes lay eggs, but in some species the female retains the eggs in her body and gives birth to fully formed young. Some species guard the eggs, but none takes any care of the young.

BREAKING FREE
A baby Burmese python breaks through its shell. It slit the shell with the tiny egg tooth that can be seen at the end of its snout and which falls off after a few days.

The egg-layers In most egg-laying species, the female looks for a safe, warm and slightly moist place—such as a rotting log, or the soil beneath a rock—to lay her eggs. Once she has laid the eggs, she covers them with soil, leaf litter or other plant matter and leaves them to develop and hatch on their own. A few species of snakes stay with the eggs until they hatch. Some pythons coil around their eggs to keep them warm and to guard them from predators. Both male and female Asian cobras have been seen digging out nest cavities and both sexes will defend the nest from predators.

The live-bearers Some snakes, such as most vipers and various species of water snakes, give birth to fully developed young. Live-bearing snakes tend to live in cold climates or water habitats. Scientists believe cool-climate snakes retain the eggs in their body because they will be warmer there than they would be in the soil, thus giving them a better chance to develop. Snakes in wet environments generally give birth to live young because eggs could easily drown in water or become moldy in wet soil.

How many? A number of factors affect how many eggs or young a snake will produce per clutch or litter. These are the size of the species; the age and size of the individual snake (young snakes lay fewer eggs than older snakes); and the availability of food, both for the mother and for the young, which may need smaller prey. Some small tropical snakes lay only a couple of eggs, probably because they produce more than one clutch per year. Most snakes, however, produce between three and 16 eggs or young per clutch or litter. A few species produce more than this, with some of the bigger snakes occasionally producing 100 offspring or more.

How often? In tropical areas some egg-laying species produce more than one clutch a year. In temperate areas, though, snakes generally produce only one clutch or litter a year because winter temperatures are too low for reproduction. Some species reproduce only every second or third year. This may be because the female does not have enough time to build up her energy stores between giving birth and the onset of winter. Or it may be that food supplies are low. The European adder and the Australian water python, for example, do not reproduce during years when rodent populations are low.

ON THEIR OWN
Neither the egg-laying snakes nor the live-bearers take any care of their young. From the moment they are hatched or born, snakes must fend for themselves. They must find their own food and they face many predators, including other snakes,

BOA CONSTRICTOR

Boas are similar in many ways to pythons except that they bear live young instead of laying eggs. The best known of the boas is the large boa constrictor *Boa constrictor*. Once thought of as a jungle snake, it is now known to be a very adaptable species and has been found in a variety of habitats from semi-deserts to rainforests. In the rainforest, it lives in the the treetops and climbs down to the ground only to look for food.

Characteristics The boa constrictor is a large snake with individuals reaching lengths of up to 20 feet (6 m), although few actually exceed 10 feet (3 m). Its colors and markings vary, but most are gray or silver with numerous large brown or deep red blotches along the back. Despite the fear inspired by the boa constrictor, it is virtually harmless to humans and, like most snakes, its first reaction to danger is to flee. If threatened it may hiss very loudly, a sound that can be heard over 100 feet (30 m) away. Boas have small teeth which slant toward the throat and prevent prey from slipping out of the mouth.

Diet The boa constrictor eats a variety of animals including birds, bats, opossums, squirrels, rats, mice

The boa constrictor can often be found near human habitation where prey such as rats, mice and sometimes a chicken or other domestic animal are easy to find.

A CLOSE RELATION
The Madagascan boa constrictor *Boa madagascariensis* is very similar to the boa constrictor. Like other boas, it kills its prey by constriction, and can attack quite large animals.

CLASSIFICATION

ORDER SQUAMATA • SUBORDER SERPENTES • C. 18 FAMILIES
C. 2,700 SPECIES • C. 450 GENERA
FAMILY BOIDAE

The growth rate of the young depends on the temperature of the environment and the availability of food, but they may double their length in the first year, maturing when they are two or three years old.

Habitat The boa constrictor is both terrestrial and arboreal and it inhabits many different habitats including semi-desert regions, open savanna, cultivated fields and wet tropical forests. It is found in Central and South America from southern Mexico to Paraguay and Argentina.

and large lizards. It cannot move very quickly, so it lies in wait for its prey or creeps up on an unsuspecting animal. Like pythons and other boas, it kills its prey by throwing its coils around the animal and tightening them each time it exhales, thus preventing it from inhaling and gradually suffocating it.

After the boa has eaten, it will lie motionless for many days while the food is digested.

Reproduction The female boa constrictor retains the unshelled eggs in her body, and gives birth to between 20 and 50 young which are about 12 inches (30 cm) long.

ANACONDA

There may be a longer python but the giant, semi-aquatic anaconda *Eunectes murinus* is without doubt the largest and heaviest of snakes, sometimes weighing more than 550 pounds (250 kg). It spends most of its time lying in wait at the water's edge for unwary mammals and caimans. During the day it basks on low branches overhanging a stream or rests in shallow water.

Characteristics The anaconda can grow to lengths of 33 feet (10 m) or more. Its dull coloring and black markings allow it to blend in well with the thick vegetation of its habitat. The nostrils are on top of its snout so it can breathe while it is swimming or lying submerged.

Diet The usual prey caught by the anaconda are turtles, caimans, birds and fish, and small mammals like deer, peccaries and large rodents.

Reproduction Like other boas, the anaconda gives birth to live young. The 20 to 40 young are 2 to 3 feet (60 cm–1 m) long when they are born.

Habitat The anaconda lives near large rivers, swamps and lakes in tropical South America, mainly in the Amazon Basin.

COOK'S TREE BOA

Cook's tree boa *Corallus enydris cookii* is one of three species of South American tree boas. All are specialized for their arboreal lifestyle, with long slender bodies and large, well-defined heads. The most spectacular of the three species is the emerald green tree boa, which is a brilliant green above with white or yellow blotches. Cook's tree boa and the garden tree boa are much duller in color.

CLASSIFICATION

ORDER SQUAMATA • SUBORDER SERPENTES • *C.* 18 FAMILIES *C.* 2,700 SPECIES • *C.* 450 GENERA FAMILY BOIDAE

Characteristics This species grows to 6½ feet (2 m) in length. There is considerable variation in color and skin pattern, ranging from dark orange, through brown to almost black. In some cases the body is distinctly patterned; other individuals have a uniform color. The underside is white spotted with gray. This boa has an unusual technique for climbing trees. It stretches upward, wraps the front of its body around the trunk and gradually pulls up the rest of its body along the tree trunk.

Diet Cook's tree boa feeds mainly on birds and small mammals such as bats, but lizards are also taken when the opportunity arises.

Reproduction Like other boas, this species bears live young. Between seven and 30 offspring are born about six months after mating.

Habitat Cook's tree boa is one of two subspecies of garden tree boas that occur in South America. This species is more common in the northern part of the range.

BRAZILIAN RAINBOW BOA

Named because of the iridescent patterned sheen of its scales, the Brazilian rainbow boa *Epicrates cenchria cenchria* feeds on the ground and is often found near village outskirts where there is a steady supply of rodents and other food. A nocturnal snake, it rests during the day in trees or on rafters in buildings.It is a stocky, rather stumpy, species, reaching up to 5 feet (1.5 m) in length.

CLASSIFICATION

ORDER SQUAMATA • SUBORDER SERPENTES • C. 18 FAMILIES C. 2,700 SPECIES • C. 450 GENERA FAMILY BOIDAE

Characteristics Although there are nine subspecies of rainbow boas, only the Brazilian rainbow boa has the bright patterning that justifies the group's common name. Between the scales bordering the upper lip, the Brazilian rainbow boa has heat-sensitive pits that are used to detect warm-blooded prey.

Diet The Brazilian rainbow boa spends part of its time in trees, but feeds on the ground. Favored prey includes a variety of small mammals, lizards and birds.

Reproduction Like other boas, this is a viviparous snake. The female retains the developing eggs within her oviduct until fully formed and gives birth to live young.

Habitat Rainbow boas are widespread through continental South America and the southern part of Central America.

SAND BOAS

The 10 species of African and Asian sand boas of the genus *Eryx* are burrowing snakes that are rarely seen above ground during the daytime. They are well adapted for their burrowing lifestyle. They dig their way through sand or loose soil with their blunt, shovel-shaped snout. In some species the eyes are on top of the head so they can see when they are partially buried.

CLASSIFICATION

ORDER SQUAMATA • SUBORDER SERPENTES • C. 18 FAMILIES C. 2,700 SPECIES • C. 450 GENERA FAMILY BOIDAE

Characteristics Sand boas rarely exceed 3 feet (1 m) and most are about half this length. They have thick, cylindrical bodies and a blunt tail. Raising this tail so it looks like a head, thus distracting a predator's attention away from the real head, is the snake's main method of defense.

Diet Small rodents, birds and lizards are favored prey Sand boas can be quick to seize and kill prey..

Reproduction Like all boas, the sand boas give birth to live young.

Habitat Sand boas are found in the arid regions of Africa and western Asia with one species, the javelin sand boa, in south-eastern Europe.

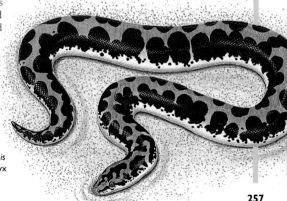

The boa in this group found the furthest south is the Kenyan sand boa Eryx colubrinus loveridgei.

257

FOOD AND FEEDING

All snakes are carnivores. They eat only animals, their young and their eggs. Some snakes have quite a broad diet, eating almost anything they can catch and subdue. Others have a very specialized diet and will eat only one thing, like snails, frogs or fish eggs. Snakes also have different ways of catching their food. Some stalk or pursue their prey. Others wait for it to come to them.

COMING UNHINGED
The bones of a snake's jaw (and some of the bones in its skull) are attached by elastic connections that allow the bones to move apart and stretch the snake's mouth wide open so it can swallow prey that is larger than its head. In fact, an adult python can eat an animal that is twice as big as its own head in diameter.

Preparing dinner Snakes have a number of ways of overcoming their prey. Snakes like boas and pythons, which eat mainly mammals, kill by constriction. They seize the animal with their sharp teeth, then wrap their coils around it, squeezing it until it suffocates. The venomous snakes inject their prey with venom which paralyzes or kills it. Some snakes swallow small animals live. They suffocate after a few minutes in the snake's stomach.

Swallowing dinner Snakes swallow their meals whole. Their sharp, inwardly curving teeth are not used for chewing but to hold prey and to maneuver it into their throat. Some snakes, like the wormsnakes, eat very large numbers of small prey items, like ants or worms. But most snakes eat a single animal, often a large one. They "walk" their

A big python "walks" its jaws over a wild pig.

wide open jaws over the prey, gradually edging it into the throat until the contractions of the gullet carry it into the stomach. The opening to the windpipe can be moved to one side so the snake can breathe while it is engaged in subduing and swallowing prey, a process that can take many hours.

A meal goes a long way

Because they can eat such huge meals relative to their size, and have a slow metabolism, snakes can survive for long periods without feeding. Compared with other animals of similar weight, snakes eat infrequently—on average once or twice a week and some only a few times a year. Digesting such meals can take weeks or even months.

After a large meal, most snakes seek a sunny, sheltered spot. Heat from the sun raises the snake's body temperature, thus providing energy to digest the food.

The smooth green snake Ophedryas vernalis *from North America eats grasshoppers, crickets and caterpillars.*

FILESNAKES

The three totally aquatic filesnakes are among the most unusual of snakes. Their skin is loose and baggy and looks as though it is one or two sizes too big for the snake. When you see a filesnake underwater, however, this strange skin makes sense. It straightens out beneath the underside of the snake, giving it a flattened profile like that of a sea snake and allowing it to swim more efficiently.

Characteristics The skin of the filesnakes is covered with small granular scales like the surface of a file. They have lost the large scales on their belly that characterize most snakes and have trouble moving about on land. The snakes have a flap in the roof of their mouth that can be used to close their nostrils and they have salt glands under their tongue. Filesnakes are mainly nocturnal and generally exist on low rates of energy. They eat rarely, are mostly slow and sluggish, and the females may reproduce only once every few years. The name given to the Asian filesnake *Acrochordus javanicus*, "Elephant's trunk snake," aptly describes all these snakes.

The average length of the little filesnake Acrochordus granulatus is about 20 inches (50 cm). It hunts for fish, crabs and other crustaceans in intertidal areas.

Diet Filesnakes feed mainly on fish, constricting them in the same way that pythons or boas constrict their prey. It is the roughened texture of their skin that enables them to hang onto and squeeze slippery fish.

Reproduction The females retain the eggs in their body until they are ready to hatch. The largest snakes give birth to between 25 and 35 live young in a single litter.

Habitat The filesnake lives in rivers and freshwater billabongs in Australia and New Guinea. The elephant's trunk snake, also a freshwater species, inhabits rivers in South-East Asia. The third species, the little filesnake, can be found in estuaries and coastal waters in the Indian and Pacific oceans.

A LARGE MEAL
At 5 feet (1.5 m) in length, the Arafuan filesnake *Acrochordus arafurae* is the largest of the filesnakes. In tropical Australia, Aboriginal people harvest these snakes to eat just before the beginning of the annual monsoon season when water levels are low. They catch the snakes by groping around in the muddy water until they feel their rough skin. The snakes are cooked by being thrown on hot campfire coals.

CLASSIFICATION

ORDER SQUAMATA • SUBORDER SERPENTES • C. 18 FAMILIES C. 2,700 SPECIES • C. 450 GENERA FAMILY ACROCHORDIDAE

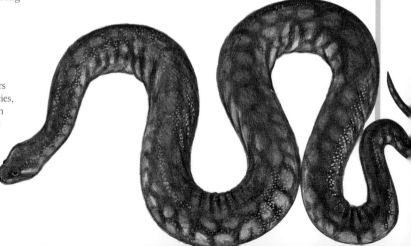

SPOTTED HARLEQUIN SNAKE

The spotted harlequin snake *Homoroselaps lacteus* of South Africa is a venomous snake often found in old termite mounds, under stones or in other secure hiding places It generally grows to 12–16 inches (30–40 cm) in length, although a maximum size of 22 inches (55 cm) has been recorded. While its venom is poisonous to humans, few bites have been recorded because of its small gape and reluctance to attack without provocation.

CLASSIFICATION

ORDER SQUAMATA • SUBORDER SERPENTES • C. 18 FAMILIES C. 2,700 SPECIES • C. 450 GENERA FAMILY COLUBRIDAE

Characteristics This small, slender snake varies in its color phases. The back can be yellowish with numerous broken black bands and orange or yellow stripes, or it may be black with irregular yellow-white crossbars and red to orange spots.

Diet The spotted harlequin snake feeds on blind snakes, legless lizards and other snakes, but rarely feeds in captivity.

Reproduction Up to six eggs are laid in a single clutch in December.

Habitat This snake is found in varied habitats, from semi-desert to savanna and coastal bushland in southern Africa.

SLUG-EATING SNAKES

The common name of these Asian snakes comes from the fact that they feed on snails. They have an elongated lower jaw which can be inserted into the opening of a snail's shell. The long front teeth then hook into the snail's soft body which the snake drags out with twisting movements. The snake does not consume the snail's shell, which it probably could not digest anyway.

CLASSIFICATION

ORDER SQUAMATA • SUBORDER SERPENTES • C. 18 FAMILIES C. 2,700 SPECIES • C. 450 GENERA FAMILY COLUBRIDAE

Characteristics Slug-eating snakes belong to the large Colubridae family, in which about 1,600 species are recognized. They are quite small, growing 18–20 inches (45–50 cm) in length, with undistinguished color of gray to brown, sometimes with darker crossbars.

Diet These snakes eat only snails and slugs of varying kinds.

Reproduction Although we know they are oviparous, little more is known of the breeding habits of these snakes.

Habitat Slug-eating snakes are common in parts of Asia, occupying habitats from sea level to mountains. They can be found in gardens and around cultivated areas as well as more remote areas, whose isolation makes them difficult to study.

Pareas formosensis *is one of several specialized slug-eating snakes found in the Asian region.*

263

VINE SNAKES

These long, thin snakes are called vine snakes because, when draped over a branch, that's just what they look like. This provides them with excellent camouflage but their length also helps them to bridge the gaps when moving from branch to branch. They are amazing climbers and can go up a vertical tree trunk without coiling around it. They simply utilize crevices in the bark for purchase. There are two groups of vine snakes: one in Latin America (genus *Oxybelis*) and another, sometimes called the twig snakes, in Africa (genus *Thelotornis*).

Characteristics Vine snakes are superbly adapted to their arboreal habitat, with narrow pointed heads, large eyes and long slender bodies. The American vine snakes grow to about 7 feet (2 m) but their body is no more than half an inch (1.2 cm) round, enabling them to blend into the branches and foliage of trees. The twig snakes grow to about 5 feet (1.5 m), almost half of which is

ENTWINED IN VINES
The slender body of the vine snake of Central and South America enables it to move rapidly across branches in search of prey such as small birds in nests.

the tail. Both groups are rear-fanged snakes. The twig snakes are highly venomous and have caused human fatalities. When threatened by a predator, a twig snake will inflate the loose skin on its chin and throat to make itself look bigger.

Diet Twig snakes feed on lizards and small birds, which they often take from nests. The American vine snakes eat mainly lizards but they will also feed on birds and small mammals.

Reproduction
Vine snakes are all egg-layers, but there is considerable variety between species in the number of eggs, nesting preferences and gestation times.

Habitat Both groups of vine snakes are highly arboreal. The American vine snakes live in low bushes, and are found in Central and South America. One species occurs in southern Arizona. The twig snakes live in the trees of the rainforests and savannas of Africa.

CLASSIFICATION

ORDER SQUAMATA • SUBORDER SERPENTES • C. 18 FAMILIES C. 2,700 SPECIES • C. 450 GENERA FAMILY COLUBRIDAE

It is thought that the twig snake Thelotornis capensis *uses its black-tipped red tongue to lure birds.*

265

HOUSE SNAKES

These nocturnal snakes earned their common name from their habit of entering houses to search for food, usually rodents or other reptiles. There are 13 species in the genus *Lamprophis,* all of which are found in southern Africa. Most are terrestrial, although some live underground in abandoned termite nests and others forage in rock crevices.

CLASSIFICATION

ORDER SQUAMATA • SUBORDER SERPENTES • C. 18 FAMILIES C. 2,700 SPECIES • C. 450 GENERA FAMILY COLUBRIDAE

Characteristics House snakes are small to medium in size, with few being larger than 3 feet (1 m) in length. In common with other nocturnal snakes, their eyes are small and their pupils vertical. Their scales are smooth, and the number of scales varies according to species. The most common species is the quite large brown house snake *Lamprophis fuliginosus,* which is found throughout most of Africa.

Lamprophis guttatus, the spotted house snake, is endemic to the arid regions of the inland mountains of the Cape, Its blotched color varies according to region.

Diet Mice and rats are the preferred food, although smaller reptiles are also taken. Some species even forage for bats.

Reproduction House snakes are oviparous and lay clutches of oval white eggs. The number and gestation period vary.

Habitat Thirteen species are found in Africa, with two species isolated in Arabia and on the Seychelles Islands. Seven species are confined to southern Africa.

WHITE-BELLIED MANGROVE SNAKE

On the mangrove mudflats at night, the white-bellied mangrove snake *Fordonia leucobalia* stalks crabs left behind by the receding tide. When the snake is close enough, it strikes the crab from above, pushing it into the soft mud with its forebody. Here the snake immobilizes the crab with its venom, then proceeds to eat it, biting off its legs and claws before consuming the rest of the crab.

CLASSIFICATION

ORDER SQUAMATA • SUBORDER SERPENTES • C. 18 FAMILIES C. 2,700 SPECIES • C. 450 GENERA FAMILY COLUBRIDAE

Characteristics This mildly venomous, rear-fanged snake grows to about 2 feet (60 cm) in length. It has a broad head with a round snout and a thin neck. Its color varies between individuals, ranging from black and dark brown to reddish brown and cream, though the belly is always pure white. Some have blotches, spots or bands on their back; others do not.

Diet The snake will eat fish, but it feeds almost entirely on crustaceans, especially crabs.

Reproduction The white-bellied mangrove snake gives birth to live young. There are usually between five and 10 in a litter.

Habitat This semi-aquatic snake lives in coastal mangroves. It shelters in crab burrows and amongst the root tangles of the mangroves, and hunts for its crustacean prey on the mudflats and in the murky tidal channels. It is found around tidal creeks and estuaries in northern Australia, New Guinea and South-East Asia.

HOW SNAKES MOVE

When snakes evolved from their lizard ancestors, they gradually lost their limbs, perhaps to take advantage of narrow spaces where limbs were not of much use. Without limbs, however, they had to evolve new ways of moving. Their very long, supple bodies provided the solution.

Large pythons, boas and vipers often use rectilinear locomotion when creeping up to prey across open ground.

Using lateral undulation, snakes can travel at speeds of up to 6 miles (10 km) per hour.

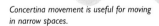

Concertina movement is useful for moving in narrow spaces.

The serpent body Snakes have a very long, very flexible backbone. Humans have just 32 vertebrae in their spine whereas some snakes have 400 or more. The vertebrae are tightly connected and reinforced to provide stability, and a complex system of interlocking muscles makes the backbone very supple. Snakes lever themselves along on the edge of their belly scales, pushing with tiny muscles attached to the ribs that are in turn attached to the vertebrae.

Lateral undulation This is the most familiar method of snake locomotion. The snake moves by pushing its side curves against the surface it is traveling on. This anchors the snake so it can push forward. Snakes often travel quite rapidly using this movement. Sea snakes also use lateral undulation. They push against the water with the sides of their curved bodies. Their flattened, oar-like tails give them extra "push."

Rectilinear locomotion When using this technique, aptly described as the "caterpillar crawl," the snake anchors its belly scales to the ground then pulls itself forward by contracting its muscles. It then pulls the belly scales forward to a new position and repeats the process. This anchoring and pushing takes place simultaneously at different segments of the body.

Concertina movement With this technique, and sidewinding, the snake uses a point of contact with the ground as purchase, then lifts its trunk clear of the ground to establish another point of contact. Sidewinding is particularly well suited to soft surfaces such as sand and mud.

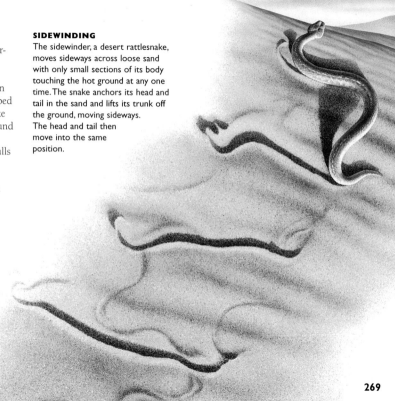

SIDEWINDING
The sidewinder, a desert rattlesnake, moves sideways across loose sand with only small sections of its body touching the hot ground at any one time. The snake anchors its head and tail in the sand and lifts its trunk off the ground, moving sideways. The head and tail then move into the same position.

COMMON GRASS SNAKE

The common grass snake *Natrix natrix* is widespread over much
of Europe, even at high latitudes. Like many species from temperate
regions, it spends the winter hibernating in holes in the ground.
In the warmer months, it is active during the day and may often
be seen basking on logs or the bank of a stream. It is never
far from water and is an excellent swimmer. It can also
climb, and sometimes goes up into the branches of
shrubs or low trees.

WIDESPREAD SPECIES
As its common name implies, this
grass snake is widely distributed
throughout Europe. It has adjusted
to human settlement, and in colder
climates takes advantage of cow
manure, in which its eggs are laid
to conserve heat.

Characteristics The common grass snake grows to around 2½ to 3 feet (76 cm–1 m) in length. It is brown, gray or olive green in color with black bars along its sides. Around its neck is a broken collar of orange, yellow, pink or white. If a predator cannot be put off by hissing and mock-striking, the grass snake defends itself by giving off a foul smell or, as a last resort, playing dead.

Diet Grass snakes eat mainly fish, frogs and newts. They will also eat lizards, birds and small mammals such as mice, shrews and voles. Tadpoles are the preferred prey of the young.

Reproduction The grass snake lays an average clutch of 30–40 eggs. Egg-laying snakes are not usually able to survive severely cold regions because the eggs need high temperatures to develop. Female grass snakes overcome this problem by migrating long distances to find suitable incubation sites. The snakes in areas as far north as Sweden lay their eggs in cow manure piles on farms. The heat caused by decomposition allows the eggs to complete their development before the first frosts of winter. Snakes from a wide area may converge on a single farm and lay thousands of eggs in one manure pile.

Habitat Grass snakes usually live near ponds and streams, or in marshy areas or damp woodlands. Some extend into drier areas. They are found in most of Europe, except for Ireland, the Balearics, Malta, Crete and some of the Cyclades.

CLASSIFICATION

ORDER SQUAMATA • SUBORDER SERPENTES • C. 18 FAMILIES C. 2,700 SPECIES • C. 450 GENERA FAMILY COLUBRIDAE

271

WATER SNAKES

The water snakes of North America are often seen basking on logs or rocks at the water's edge, or in branches overhanging a stream. All are good swimmers, though some prefer slow-moving water. They search for their prey in the vegetation along the shoreline or hunt for it in the water. Water snakes have been seen fishing with their mouth open to the current, grabbing any fish that swims by.

CLASSIFICATION

ORDER SQUAMATA • SUBORDER SERPENTES • C. 18 FAMILIES C. 2,700 SPECIES • C. 450 GENERA FAMILY COLUBRIDAE

Characteristics These snakes vary in length from around 15 inches (38 cm) to over 4 feet (1.2 m). They are usually dark brown, gray or black with lighter undersides. Escape is their main method of defense, but if cornered they will bite, or emit foul smells or excrement.

The northern water snake Nerodia sipedon is active day and night. It catches fish in the shallows and and hunts for frogs, like this unlucky carpenter frog, at the water's edge. It gives birth to an average of between 20 and 40 live young.

Diet Water snakes eat fish, frogs, tadpoles, salamanders, young turtles and crustaceans.

Reproduction All water snakes give birth to live young and have a placenta to nourish the embryos.

Habitat These snakes are found in or near most aquatic habitats: rivers, streams, lakes, swamps, ponds, marshes, ditches, bogs and canals. They are common and widely distributed throughout North America.

RIBBON AND GARTER SNAKES

The semi-aquatic ribbon snakes are rarely found far from water. They like to bask in the bushes on the shoreline, but if startled will take to the water. Unlike water snakes which dive, ribbon snakes glide swiftly across the water's surface. Ribbon snakes are almost always found in low, wet places like swamps and marshes, or the weedy margins of lakes, ponds and quiet streams and rivers. They prefer shallow water.

CLASSIFICATION

ORDER SQUAMATA • SUBORDER SERPENTES • C. 18 FAMILIES C. 2,700 SPECIES • C. 450 GENERA FAMILY COLUBRIDAE

Characteristics Active during the day, ribbon snakes have large eyes and round pupils. They have a slender, streamlined body, ranging from 18 inches (45 cm) to 4 feet (1.2 m) in length. About a third of that length is the very long, thin tail.

Diet Ribbon snakes eat small fish, frogs, tadpoles, salamanders and earthworms.

Reproduction Ribbon snakes give birth to live young, with litter sizes varying between three and twenty-seven. The newborn young are about 10 inches (25 cm) long.

Habitat Ribbon snakes live on the margins of streams, swamps, ditches and lakes in North and Central America.

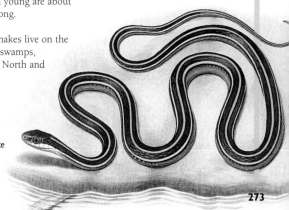

The eastern ribbon snake Thamnophis sauritus eats frogs, salamanders and minnows.

273

RIBBON AND GARTER SNAKES

Garter snakes are common throughout North America. The most widely distributed species, the common garter snake *Thamnophis sirtalis*, is found from warm regions in the south where it is active all year through to severely cold areas in Canada. Here huge groups gather together to spend the winter in the few sites where underground crevices are deep enough for them to escape the winter freeze.

Due to the destruction of its habitat through residential and industrial development, the San Francisco garter snake Thamnophis sirtalis tetrataenia *is an endangered species.*

Characteristics Most garter snakes have light stripes on a dark background running the length of their bodies. Many also have some spots, usually on or around the head. Garter snakes are active during the day when they bask and hunt for food. When cornered, some species will bite and emit foul smells.

Diet As a group, garter snakes eat a wide range of food. Different species eat different things, even if they are found in the same area, perhaps because of competition between species. The most common prey items are small fish (often minnows), frogs, salamanders and earthworms. Also eaten are tadpoles, leeches, slugs, insects, insect larvae, birds and small rodents such as mice.

Reproduction The females retain the eggs inside their body and give birth to live young. At the time of birth, some may still be covered in a thin membrane, which they soon

A coast garter snake Thamnophis elegans terrestris. *Garter snakes do not engage in male-to-male combat in search of a reproductive mate. Large size, therefore, does not appear to be a significant advantage, and most garter snakes of both sexes are relatively slight.*

burst. Litter sizes vary enormously, from four or five up to a hundred.

Habitat Garter snakes inhabit all sorts of environments, from deserts to forests, from mountain slopes to the coast, but they are semi-aquatic and are always found near water. They live on the margins of lakes, streams, ponds, marshes, swamps, drainage ditches and irrigation canals. They are common and widely distributed throughout North America, from Costa Rica to southern Canada.

The western garter snake Thamnophis couchi, *like other species in the genus, is adapted to a semi-aquatic life.*

HOGNOSE SNAKES

These heavily built snakes have a remarkable defense display. When threatened, they flatten their neck and head in a cobra-like pose, inflate their body, and hiss and strike vigorously. If this formidable display fails to deter the attacker, the snake turns onto its back and feigns death with its mouth open and its tongue hanging out. The snakes are active in the daytime and burrow deep into loose earth in the winter.

CLASSIFICATION

ORDER SQUAMATA • SUBORDER SERPENTES • C. 18 FAMILIES
C. 2,700 SPECIES • C. 450 GENERA
FAMILY COLUBRIDAE

The eastern hognose snake Heterodon platyrhinos *is sometimes called a puff adder.*

Characteristics Hognose snakes have a stout body, broad head, wide neck and a slightly upturned, pointed and shovel-shaped snout. They range in length from about 15 inches (38 cm) to 33 inches (84 cm).

Diet These snakes feed primarily on toads. They use their broad snouts to dig their prey out of burrows. If the toad tries to defend itself by inflating its body, the snake punctures it with its large back teeth. There is a mild venom in these teeth that subdues the snake's prey.

Reproduction Hognose snakes lay clutches of between four and 60 eggs, with 15–25 being more typical.

Habitat These snakes live in a wide variety of habitats including open sandy areas, grasslands, thinly wooded areas and rocky, semi-arid lands. They are found in southern Canada, the USA and Mexico.

FALSE VIPERS

The markings and behavior of this group of Latin American snakes are similar to those of several terrestrial pit vipers that live in the same area. They are fairly sedentary snakes and feed mainly on toads. At the back of their mouth they have enlarged teeth which they use to puncture the toads when they inflate themselves. If threatened, these snakes flatten their neck and body so they look more intimidating.

Characteristics Active day or night, the false vipers have round eyes with large pupils.

Diet These snakes feed largely on toads and frogs.

Reproduction False vipers lay clutches of 15–25 eggs.

Habitat The false vipers are usually found near water. They live on the banks of rivers in rainforests from Mexico to Argentina.

CLASSIFICATION

***ORDER* SQUATA • *SUBORDER* SERPENTES** • *C.* 18 FAMILIES *C.* 2,700 SPECIES • *C.* 450 GENERA **FAMILY** COLUBRIDAE

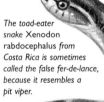

The toad-eater snake Xenodon rabdocephalus *from Costa Rica is sometimes called the false fer-de-lance, because it resembles a pit viper.*

SNAKE SENSES

Snakes have all the usual senses, plus some extra ones as well. They rely on a variety of sense organs to detect their prey, recognize a predator and find a mate, but smell is probably the most important of these senses. The snake's forked tongue is a superb instrument for gathering information about chemicals in its environment.

The eyelash pit viper Bothriechis schlegeli *of Central and South America uses the heat- sensitive pits near its eyes to detect prey.*

The flicking tongue A snake flicks its tongue to pick up particles from the air, water or the ground. When it withdraws the tongue into the mouth, it brings these particles to the Jacobson's organ which is in the roof of the mouth. There the chemical molecules are analyzed, giving the snake accurate information about the presence of predators or prey. In this way, the Jacobson's organ has a similar function to the taste and smell organs of humans.

Eyesight Snakes' eyesight varies enormously between species. Some, like the wormsnakes, can only distinguish light and dark, whereas some of the day-active terrestrial and tree-dwelling snakes have very acute vision. These diurnal snakes usually have large eyes. Some nocturnal snakes have small eyes, but many

ON THE LOOKOUT
An East African bush snake
Philothamnus sp. These diurnal snakes have
slender green bodies with large eyes and
round pupils. They are agile snakes and
use a combination of senses to locate and
kill their prey of small vertebrates,
particularly amphibians.

have vertical pupils which open up
wide in dim light. Snakes do not
have moveable eyelids. Rather the
eyes of most species are covered by
transparent caps, called brilles. This
gives them their unblinking stare, so
often interpreted as a sign of
malevolent intentions.

Hearing It was once thought that
snakes were totally deaf because they
have no external ear openings.
However, most snakes have a well-
developed inner ear and it is now
known that they are capable of
detecting even faint vibrations through
the ground or water. Recent research

suggests that some snakes may be able
to hear airborne sounds as well.

Heat pits Pit vipers and most
pythons and boas have special
sensory organs that detect infrared
heat rays. These organs are situated
in pits on the side of the face of the
pit vipers and on the lips of pythons
and boas. With these heat receptors,
a snake can detect warm-blooded
prey because of the slight difference
in temperature between the prey and

its surroundings. It can also detect
how far away the animal is and
where its heart (its warmest part) is
located. Thus the snake can strike
accurately, even in total darkness.

Which sense? Snakes use a
combination of all their senses to
find their prey. Scientists still have
much to learn about the way in
which information received via the
different senses is combined and
interpreted in the snake's brain.

KING SNAKES

Like the king cobra, king snakes earned their name from their habit of eating other snakes. Completely non-venomous, they kill their prey by constricting and suffocating it. They are terrestrial snakes, though some will occasionally climb into shrubs. Most are active in the early morning and at dusk but some species are secretive nocturnal creatures that spend most of the day in burrows.

CLASSIFICATION

ORDER SQUAMATA • *SUBORDER SERPENTES* • *C.* 18 FAMILIES *C.* 2,700 SPECIES • *C.* 450 GENERA **FAMILY** COLUBRIDAE

Characteristics The color and patterns of king snakes vary greatly. Some are spectacularly colorful with red, white and black bands. Others have alternating black and white to yellowish bands and some are all black. The king snake is regarded as a gentle snake, but if threatened it will hiss loudly, strike out and vibrate its tail.

Diet As well as other snakes, king snakes eat small rodents, birds, eggs, frogs, lizards and turtles.

Reproduction The female lays a clutch of two to 25 eggs in a cavity in the soil and covers them with leaf and plant litter.

Habitat King snakes live in many habitats, from forests to grasslands to deserts. They are found in the USA, Mexico, Central America and northern South America.

The common king snake Lampropeltis getulus is famous for eating rattlesnakes, coral snakes and copperheads. It has anti-toxins in its blood that make it immune to the venom of these snakes.

MILK SNAKE

One of the most colorful snakes in the king snake genus is the milk snake. Its common name comes from the myth that it entered barns and sucked the milk from cows. A secretive snake, it is usually not seen in the open in daylight hours when it hides away under rotting logs or stumps or in damp rubbish piles. When threatened, it will either coil up and hide its head, or vibrate its tail and strike.

CLASSIFICATION

ORDER SQUAMATA • SUBORDER SERPENTES • C. 18 FAMILIES C. 2,700 SPECIES • C. 450 GENERA FAMILY COLUBRIDAE

Characteristics There are several subspecies of this snake with varied colors and markings. Some have bright red, black and yellow bands. The average length of the snake is around 30 inches (75 cm).

Diet These snakes eat a variety of prey including rodents, birds, lizards and other snakes. A milk snake can easily enter a mammal burrow where it takes the young from their nest. Milk snakes also occasionally eat frogs, fish, earthworms, slugs and insects.

Reproduction In the summer the female lays a clutch of between two and 17 eggs. She will often lay the eggs in a rotten log.

Habitat Milk snakes inhabit many areas including forests, woodlands, cultivated land, prairies, sand dunes, even vacant lots in urban areas. They are found in the USA, Mexico, and Central and northern South America.

This eastern milk snake Lampropeltis triangulum triangulum is an albino without the usual black bands of the species.

RAT SNAKES

The rat snakes are powerful, non-venomous constrictors that feed on warm-blooded prey, particularly rodents, giving the group their common name. The snakes are mostly terrestrial, spending much of their time in burrows looking for food. Some, like the black rat snake *Elaphe obsoleta*, the most common North American rat snake, are skillful climbers and will go up into trees or the rafters of abandoned buildings looking for mice and birds and their eggs. When threatened, rat snakes will coil up and strike, with their tail vibrating rapidly.

Characteristics Some rat snakes are very large. The largest colubrid snake of all is the Asian rat snake *Ptyas mucosus* which grows to lengths of over 11 feet (3.5 m). The black rat snake is the longest American snake, reaching a length of well over 8 feet (2.5 m). The color and pattern of many rat snakes change as they grow and mature. Young rat snakes are often marked with large dark blotches that gradually disappear and give way to longitudinal stripes as the animal gets older. Sometimes the areas between the blotches become darker with each slough until the snake is eventually a uniform color. The snakes tend to hunt in the early morning or at

The Mandarin rat snake Elaphe mandarina *is a brilliantly colored snake from high-altitude regions in China.*

dusk. They become more nocturnal on warm summer nights.

Diet As well as rats and mice, rat snakes eat other small mammals, lizards, frogs, birds and eggs. The totally nocturnal Trans-Pecos rat snake *Bogertophis subocularis* from southern USA and Mexico also eats bats. Sometimes the snakes simply swallow smaller prey without constricting it in their coils first.

Reproduction Rat snakes lay eggs in the summer months in places such as rotten logs and stumps, in leaf litter or under rocks.

Habitat These snakes occupy a variety of habitats from rocky deserts to swamps and marshes, from coastal plains to mountains, and from forests to farmland and barnyards. They are found in the USA, Mexico, Europe and Asia.

CLASSIFICATION

ORDER SQUAMATA • SUBORDER SERPENTES • C. 18 FAMILIES C. 2,700 SPECIES • C. 450 GENERA FAMILY COLUBRIDAE

FROM THE EVERGLADES
The Everglades rat snake *Elaphe obsoleta rossalleni* is a long and powerful constrictor. Its skin is a distinctive red-orange with faint stripes. It has a red tongue. As its common name suggests, this snake inhabits the Everglades in southern Florida. It is one of six subspecies of rat snakes in the southern and eastern parts of the USA that together inhabit forest, upland, wetland and farmland in both wet and arid areas.

PINE-GOPHER SNAKES

The pine-gopher snakes of North America are large, powerful snakes that kill their prey by constriction. When threatened they try to intimidate their attacker by raising and shaking their tail and hissing loudly. They have a specially modified epiglottis which increases the volume of the hiss. Because of their coloring, the pine-gopher snakes are sometimes mistaken for rattlesnakes.

CLASSIFICATION

ORDER SQUAMATA • SUBORDER
SERPENTES • c. 18 FAMILIES
c. 2,700 SPECIES • c. 450 GENERA
FAMILY COLUBRIDAE

Characteristics These snakes usually have cream or yellow skin with black patches on their back. They have a small head with a rather pointed snout (unlike the larger, more triangular head of a rattlesnake). They range in length from 4 to 8 feet (1.2–2.5 m).

Diet Pine-gopher snakes eat rodents, rabbits, lizards, birds and their eggs, and insects.

Reproduction These snakes mate in spring and lay clutches of between three and 24 cream to white eggs.

Habitat There are 15 subspecies, occupying a wide range of habitats in the USA and through to Mexico and Baja California.

The Florida pine snake Pituophis melanoleucas mugitus *is grayish to rusty brown, with indistinct blotches.*

MANGROVE SNAKE

The strikingly marked mangrove snake *Boiga dendrophila* of South-East Asia is a nocturnal, tree-dwelling snake. It is a remarkably adept climber, and preys on birds and any other invertebrates it encounters. The mangrove snake is also known as the yellow-ringed cat snake because of the vertical slit in its eyes which resembles that of a cat.

CLASSIFICATION

ORDER SQUAMATA • SUBORDER SERPENTES • *C.* 18 FAMILIES *C.* 2,700 SPECIES • *C.* 450 GENERA FAMILY COLUBRIDAE

Characteristics The mangrove snake has a slender body that is compressed from side to side, an adaptation that suits its highly arboreal existence. A long snake, it grows to nearly 8 feet (2.5 m). At the back of its mouth it has enlarged teeth that break the skin of prey, allowing venom from the snake's salivary glands to enter the animal's bloodstream. Like many rear-fanged snakes its head is short and broad. Most rear-fanged snakes are not harmful to humans, but because of this snake's size, it can be dangerous.

Diet The mangrove snake feeds on birds, bats, lizards and also on other snakes. It pursues its prey swiftly and efficiently, swooping from its treetop vantage point.

Reproduction The mangrove snake lays eggs but little is known about its reproductive biology.

Habitat This snake inhabits lowland jungles and mangrove swamps. It is found in Indonesia, Malaysia, Singapore, Thailand, the Philippines and Vietnam.

BLUNT-HEADED TREE SNAKE

The blunt-headed tree snake *Imantodes cenchoa* is a nocturnal tree-dwelling snake with an incredibly long and slender body which is compressed from side to side. It subdues its prey with venom delivered from the fangs at the back of its mouth.

CLASSIFICATION

ORDER SQUAMATA • SUBORDER SERPENTES • C. 18 FAMILIES C. 2,700 SPECIES • C. 450 GENERA FAMILY COLUBRIDAE

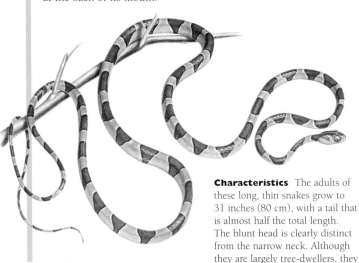

Characteristics The adults of these long, thin snakes grow to 31 inches (80 cm), with a tail that is almost half the total length. The blunt head is clearly distinct from the narrow neck. Although they are largely tree-dwellers, they sometimes descend to the ground in search of prey.

Diet These snakes are nocturnal, and forage for lizards and frogs among the tree branches.

Reproduction The blunt-headed tree snake is oviparous, laying small clutches of between one and three eggs.

Habitat This snake is distributed through Central America and northern South America.

LONG-NOSED TREE SNAKE

The long-nosed tree snake *Dryophis nasuta* is one of a small number of species that have horizontal pupils and are able to focus their eyes in a forward direction. This binocular vision allows them to focus and see better than other snakes. An exceptionally long and slender snake with green coloring, it looks like part of a tree as it lies completely motionless along a branch for hours on end, often with the front third of its body held unsupported yet rigid in space. When it spots a lizard to eat, however, it pursues it very quickly.

CLASSIFICATION

ORDER SQUAMATA • SUBORDER SERPENTES • C. 18 FAMILIES C. 2,700 SPECIES • C. 450 GENERA **FAMILY** COLUBRIDAE

Characteristics The long-nosed tree snake has large grooves which run from its eyes to its snout, allowing both eyes to look forward. It is about 4½ feet (1.4 m) in length, with nearly half this being made up by the tail. In color, it ranges from light green through to gray-brown, sometimes with light stripes on both sides. This rear-fanged snake is active during the day, and can move swiftly over ground as well as in the trees.

Diet Arboreal lizards, and occasionally frogs or young birds, eggs or small mammals make up the main part of this snake's diet.

Reproduction The long-nosed tree snake is an egg-laying species, laying clutches of between two and 12 eggs.

Habitat This species occurs in tropical rainforests. It is distributed in parts of Asia from India south to Thailand.

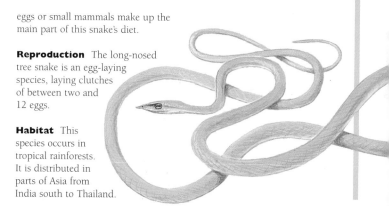

RINGNECK SNAKE

The golden ring around the neck of this snake gives it its common name. While its upper surface is dull, to match its surroundings, it has bright red or orange scales on its tail and sometimes along the length of its belly. When the snake feels threatened it will coil its tail tightly and lift it up. The sudden appearance of the bright underside can startle a predator, giving the snake time to seek cover.

CLASSIFICATION

ORDER SQUAMATA • SUBORDER SERPENTES • C. 18 FAMILIES C. 2,700 SPECIES • C. 450 GENERA FAMILY COLUBRIDAE

Characteristics The ringneck snake *Diadophis punctatus* is a small, slender snake which grows from 10 to 18 inches (25–45 cm) in length. Its dorsal coloring varies according to where it is found and can be gray, olive, brown or black. In some snakes the neck ring is either broken up or missing altogether.

Diet The ringneck snake eats earthworms, slugs, frogs, lizards, small salamanders and newborn snakes. It partly constricts its prey before eating it.

Reproduction Clutches of two to eight eggs are laid in the summer months. The females often lay their eggs in communal nesting sites and may return to the same sites, year after year.

Habitat Ringneck snakes shelter under shrubs, flat rocks, logs or the loose bark of dead trees. They prefer moist areas and live in forests, woodlands, grasslands or near the edges of streams. They are widespread throughout the USA and much of Mexico.

RACER

The racer *Coluber constrictor* is an agile snake which actively seeks its prey. When it spots an animal, it moves swiftly through the undergrowth toward it. Despite its scientific name, the racer does not kill its prey by constriction but by pressing it to the ground. When threatened, the racer may try to intimidate its attacker by vibrating its tail against the ground or amongst dead leaves to produce a sound.

CLASSIFICATION

ORDER SQUAMATA • SUBORDER SERPENTES • C. 18 FAMILIES C. 2,700 SPECIES • C. 450 GENERA FAMILY COLUBRIDAE

Characteristics Like many other fast-moving, diurnal species, the racer has large eyes with prominent pupils. It has a slender, streamlined and agile body with a rather large, angular head.

Diet Racers eat lizards, frogs, small rodents and other mammals, birds and insects.

Reproduction In the summer, the female racer lays clutches averaging between 10 and 12 eggs. The eggs are laid in rotting logs or tree stumps, in loose soil or leaf litter, or they may be laid in the burrows of small mammals like gophers and ground squirrels.

Habitat The racer lives in the brushy undergrowth of grassy areas. It is found in southern Canada, the USA, Mexico and Guatemala.

WORMSNAKES

These burrowing snakes resemble worms both in shape and, often, in color. Their eyes are just small, dark spots that can tell the difference between light and dark and probably little else. Their blunt head merges smoothly with the rest of the body, and the tail is short and tipped with a small spine that is used to anchor the snake so that it can move forward more easily as it burrows through soil.

The thread snake Leptotyphlops humilis *from Central America defends itself against the bites and stings of worker ants trying to defend their nest by secreting chemicals that repel the ants.*

Characteristics In size the wormsnakes range from less than 4 inches (10 cm) up to heavy-bodied species that reach almost 31 inches (80 cm) in length. The blindsnakes (family Typhlopidae) have teeth only on their upper jaw, while the very slender threadsnakes (family Leptotyphlopidae) have teeth only on their lower jaw. The third family, the blind wormsnakes (family Anomalepididae), have teeth on their upper jaw, with rarely more than a single tooth on the lower jaw. All the wormsnakes are non-venomous.

Diet Wormsnakes feed on worms or on the eggs and larvae of ants and termites. They rely on scent, rather than their rudimentary eyes, to locate their food. They are adept trail-followers, flicking their tongues in and out to pick up any faint chemical traces left by foraging ants. They then follow the trail back to the ant nest.

Reproduction Although a few African blindsnakes produce live young, most wormsnakes lay eggs. Unusually, the tiny flowerpot snakes are all females and they produce offspring, all female, without the presence of males.

Habitat Wormsnakes shelter in burrows in sand and soil, or under logs and rocks. They prefer moist habitats so will burrow deeper in dry times. The blindsnakes are found in Africa, Asia, Australia and Central America. The threadsnakes inhabit the USA, Central America, the West Indies, Africa, Arabia and Pakistan. The blind wormsnakes occur in Central and South America.

The flowerpot snake Ramphotyphlops braminus *has the broadest geographic range of any snake. This is almost certainly because the snake has been unwittingly spread around the globe by humans in small containers of soil, such as flowerpots.*

CLASSIFICATION

ORDER SQUAMATA • *SUBORDER SERPENTES* • *C.* 18 FAMILIES *C.* 2,700 SPECIES • *C.* 450 GENERA FAMILIES ANOMALEPIDIDAE, LEPTOTYPHLOPIDAE, TYPHLOPIDAE

VENOMOUS SNAKES

Many snakes are venomous. In the least venomous species, the venom acts only as a digestive juice, but in the most venomous snakes it is used to subdue and kill prey. There are three groups of snakes that kill their prey with venom: the rear-fanged, fixed front-fanged and swinging front-fanged snakes.

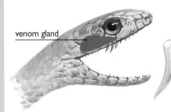

venom gland

SWINGING FRONT FANGS
All the vipers have long hollow fangs that are attached to a small bone at the front of the mouth. This bone rotates, allowing the fangs to lie back along the upper jaw when not in use.

FIXED FRONT FANGS
Snakes with fixed front fangs have hollow fangs in the front of the mouth which are firmly fixed to the upper jaw. Venom travels down the hollow fang and is injected into the prey animal.

REAR FANGS
Rear-fanged snakes have fixed fangs with grooves located toward the back of the mouth. Venom travels down the grooves along the length of the fangs.

Rear-fanged snakes Many non-venomous snakes have enlarged teeth at the back of their mouth which they use for slitting hard objects, like eggs, or puncturing prey like toads that inflate themselves so they become hard to swallow. A number of rear-fanged species, however, have potent venom. They hold their prey in the back of their mouth and chew on it so the venom enters the broken skin.

Fixed front fangs Cobras, kraits, taipans, mambas, coral snakes, sea snakes and all the Australian venomous snakes have hollow fangs in the front of the mouth which are firmly attached to the upper jaw. Most actively search for their food. When they strike, they either hang on until the venom takes effect or release their prey, which dies quickly.

Swinging front-fangs Because vipers' fangs can be folded away, they can have much longer fangs than the fixed-fang snakes. When the viper strikes, the mouth is opened wide and the fangs are swung down to stab the prey. The venom is delivered deep into the victim's body. The viper then usually releases the animal and waits for it to die.

Venom varieties Snake venoms are a complex mixture of various chemical substances and they affect prey in different ways. The neurotoxic venoms of the cobras and their relatives act on the nerves to stop the heart and damage the lungs. The hemotoxic venoms of the vipers and pit vipers cause a breakdown of the blood cells, leading to internal bleeding and the destruction of the muscles. Most venomous snakes are highly resistant to their own venom.

A rattlesnake injects a large amount of venom through its long, hollow fangs. The venom acts quickly, paralyzing or killing the prey.

RED-BELLIED BLACK SNAKE

The red-bellied black snake *Pseudechis porphyriacus* is one of eastern Australia's best known snakes. It hunts during the day and can often be seen basking at the edge of a creek or on the side of a road. The snake will flee if it feels threatened, but if cornered it will hiss loudly, flatten its neck and raise its head and upper body, cobra-like, so it looks as big as possible to an attacker.

CLASSIFICATION

ORDER SQUAMATA • SUBORDER SERPENTES • C. 18 FAMILIES
C. 2,700 SPECIES • C. 450 GENERA
FAMILY ELAPIDAE

Characteristics This is a large snake, growing to lengths of 5–6½ feet (1.5–2 m), with some individuals reaching 8 feet (2.5 m). It has a thick body and a small head. It is always a glossy purplish black on top, but its belly scales vary from pink to red. The snake is very venomous but only one human fatality has been recorded.

Diet Frogs constitute the main part of this snake's diet. It also eats small lizards, other snakes, birds, mice, rats and occasionally fish, including eels.

Reproduction The female retains the eggs in her body, giving birth to between five and 40 young. When they are born, the young are enclosed in a membrane from which they emerge soon after birth.

Habitat The snake shelters in abandoned burrows, in hollow logs or under rocks. It prefers moist habitats such as swamps, river banks, or the edges of wet forests. It is widespread along the coast of eastern Australia though the cane toad has depleted its numbers.

DEATH ADDERS

These slow-moving, terrestrial snakes have a very unusual way of catching food. With its body in a loose coil and the tip of its tail near its snout, the death adder lies motionless and half-buried in sand or leaf litter. When prey approaches, the snake wriggles the tip of its tail. As a bird or lizard moves closer to investigate the wriggling "worm" or "caterpillar," the snake strikes with lightning speed.

CLASSIFICATION

ORDER SQUAMATA • SUBORDER SERPENTES • C. 18 FAMILIES C. 2,700 SPECIES • C. 450 GENERA FAMILY ELAPIDAE

Characteristics With their broad triangular head, stocky body and thin tail, the three Australian death adders look similar to the unrelated vipers. They are highly poisonous, and capable of injecting large quantities of venom with their long fangs. They grow to between 26 and 30 inches (65–75 cm) in length. Death adders are usually active at night, especially during the warmer part of the year.

Diet Death adders eat lizards, mice, frogs and birds.

Reproduction Death adders give birth to live young, twice a year. The litters vary from a couple of young to more than thirty.

Habitat These snakes occupy a wide range of habitats from deserts to rainforests. The are found all over Australia except Tasmania, and in New Guinea.

A stocky, ambush predator, the common death adder Acanthophis antarcticus is the most widespread of the three Australian death adders.

COBRAS

These African and Asian snakes are famous for the pose they adopt when they are threatened or disturbed. They rear up and spread the loose skin on their neck into a "hood." This is done by extending the thin neck ribs behind the head. Most cobras are not aggressive and will merely lunge at their attacker. The three spitting cobras, however, will spray venom at the eyes of an intruder.

SPITTING COBRAS

In most snakes, venom pours out of the open tip of their hollow fangs. But by exhaling forcefully, a spitting cobra sprays it out in a jet, like water spraying from a puncture in a hose, and can hit a target nearly 10 feet (3 m) away.

Characteristics The king cobra *Ophiophagus hannah* of Asia is the largest venomous snake in the world, reaching more than 16 feet (5 m) in length. Its head can be as large as a man's hand. The smallest cobra is the African burrowing cobra *Paranaja multifasciata* which grows to 2 feet (60 cm). The Indian cobra *Naja naja naja* grows to about 5 feet (1.5 m) and is sometimes called the spectacled cobra because of the black and white eyeglass pattern on the back of its head. Cobras vary in color, from yellow to brown and black. They have quite short fangs attached to their upper jaws through which their venom is delivered.

Diet Cobras eat frogs, lizards, rats, birds and their eggs, and fish. The king cobra feeds primarily on other snakes, including venomous species. The African water cobra *Boulengerina annulata* emerges from boulders on the shore of the great freshwater lakes at dusk to hunt for fish. To catch prey, a cobra strikes upward with its snout curled back so that it can sink its fangs into the animal's body and inject it with venom.

Reproduction All cobras lay eggs except the rhingal *Hemachatus haemachatus*, an African spitting cobra which gives birth to live young. Asian cobras guard the eggs. The king cobra builds the most complex nest of all the snakes. The female scrapes together a large pile of grass, leaves and soil, and makes a cavity in the top of the pile where she lays the eggs. She then covers the clutch with more leaves and guards the eggs until they hatch.

Habitat With the exception of the forest cobra *Naja melanoleuca*, which lives in African rainforests, cobras prefer open habitats like savannas and grasslands. They are often found near areas of human habitation. Cobras are found in Africa, the Middle East and Asia.

CLASSIFICATION

ORDER SQUAMATA • SUBORDER SERPENTES • *C.* 18 FAMILIES *C.* 2,700 SPECIES • *C.* 450 GENERA **FAMILY** ELAPIDAE

The monacled cobra Naja naja kaouthia *is found in lowlands from western India to south-west China.*

MAMBAS

While tales of their speed and aggressiveness are highly exaggerated, there is no doubt that the black mamba is among the most dangerous of all the snakes. The threat display of an angry mamba—head and neck held high, black mouth gaping open—is a truly terrifying sight. It is also probably the swiftest of snakes when chasing its prey through the undergrowth.

CLASSIFICATION

ORDER SQUAMATA • SUBORDER SERPENTES • c. 18 FAMILIES c. 2,700 SPECIES • c. 450 GENERA FAMILY ELAPIDAE

Characteristics The color of the black mamba varies from olive brown to a dark pewter or gunmetal gray. The three other mamba species are all arboreal snakes, and predominantly green in color. All four species have long slender bodies and coffin-shaped heads.

Diet Mambas eat small mammals, especially rodents, lizards and birds. Active predators, they can just pluck a bird out of the air.

The black mamba Dendroaspis polylepis is the largest mamba, reaching lengths of 14 feet (4.3 m).

They differ from most snakes in that they strike their prey and then wait for it to die before eating it.

Reproduction Mambas lay an average of around 12 eggs. The black mamba usually lays her eggs in a moist, unused mammal burrow.

Habitat The mainly terrestrial black mamba usually inhabits rocky or open bush country. The three tree-dwelling species live in thick bush or forest or rainforest. Mambas are found only in Africa.

CORAL SNAKES

These brightly colored snakes have extremely potent venom. Their startling bands of red, black, yellow and white warn predators to stay away, and some predatory birds have an innate fear of the colors. Some coral snakes defend themselves by hiding their head and waving their tail in the air like a head. Any predator seizing this "head" is likely to receive an unpleasant surprise when the real one appears.

CLASSIFICATION

ORDER SQUAMATA • SUBORDER SERPENTES • C. 18 FAMILIES C. 2,700 SPECIES • C. 450 GENERA FAMILY ELAPIDAE

Characteristics The coral snakes are small and slender. The largest grows to about 5 feet (1.5 m). They have short fangs, fixed to their upper jaw, and small heads.

Diet Most species forage for prey on the forest floor. Lizards and other snakes are their main food, but some species also take mammals, birds, frogs and invertebrates.

Reproduction Coral snakes lay eggs but little else is known about their reproductive biology.

Habitat Some species are aquatic but most are secretive, terrestrial snakes that spend much of their time in tunnels below the ground or under rocks and logs. They are found mainly in the tropical regions of South America as well as in Central America and southern USA.

If the warning colors of the Arizona coral snake Microuroides euryxanthus euryxanthus *fail to deter a predator, it will hide its head, raise its tail and make a popping sound by turning its cloacal lining outward.*

299

DEFENSE TACTICS

Like a frill-necked lizard, this harmless vine snake opens it brightly colored mouth wide to startle a predator.

Because snakes are predatory, often feared, animals, it is often forgotten that they, too, are preyed upon. Snakes are killed and eaten by a number of animals—fish, lizards, other snakes, birds of prey and mammals—and so they have evolved a number of ways of defending themselves.

FALSE COLORS
The bright bands of color on some venomous snakes, like the Mayan coral snake *Micrurus puta mayensis* (top), warn predators away. The almost identical colors of non-venomous snakes, like the false coral snake *Erythrolamprus* sp. (below), trick predators into staying away from them too.

Staying hidden The best defense a snake can have is to avoid being seen and so they rarely stray far from cover. Some have colors and patterns that provide excellent camouflage as well. If they stay very still, an approaching enemy will not see them.

Flight first The first instinct of most snakes is to flee from danger. Many, especially the slender-bodied species, depend on speed for escape, moving quickly into the cover of a burrow or up into a tree. These snakes can move quite quickly over short distances.

Intimidation If escape is not possible, some snakes will attempt to intimidate their attacker. Some do this by expanding parts of their body so they look bigger and more formidable. Some snakes have brightly colored mouths which they open wide to frighten a predator. Others hiss loudly, or make other noises by vibrating their tail against

IN HIDING
Camouflage is one of the most effective ways by which snakes can avoid predators and lie in wait for prey. The colors and patterns of snake skin are often similar to the varied habitats they frequent. Other species have brightly colored skin whose color signals danger to predators.

Cobras flatten their heads and necks horizontally to make themselves look more intimidating.

dry leaves or, in the case of the rattlesnakes, buzzing their tail.

Fooling the enemy Some snakes wave their tail to distract attention away from their more vulnerable head. While their attacker goes for their tail, the snake has time to work out an escape route. This tactic is used by a number of the burrowing pythons and boas, which bear scars on their tails that prove it works. Playing dead is another tactic used to trick predators. The North American hog-nose snakes and the European grass snake will turn over and pretend to be dead as a last line of defense.

SEA KRAITS

The sea kraits are brightly banded marine snakes of the Indo-Pacific region. They have highly toxic venom but are extremely reluctant to bite, even in self-defense. They spend much of their time ashore on small coral islands where they seek shelter, bask in the sun, and lay their eggs.

CLASSIFICATION

ORDER SQUAMATA • SUBORDER SERPENTES • *c.* 18 FAMILIES *c.* 2,700 SPECIES • *c.* 450 GENERA **FAMILY** ELAPIDAE

can close their nostrils with fleshy valves when they are underwater. They grow to about 5 feet (1.5 m) in length and are fixed-front-fang snakes.

Diet Some species feed almost exclusively on eels, but others eat a variety of fish species.

Reproduction Sea kraits lay their eggs on coral islands, often in caves above the tideline.

Characteristics

Sea kraits have a specialized, flattened, paddle-like tail for swimming, but have retained their cylindrical shape and enlarged belly scales for crawling on land. They

Habitat One sea krait, *Laticauda crockeri*, is restricted to a landlocked lake in the Solomon Islands, but the other five species are truly marine. They are found near river mouths, mangrove swamps and in the shallow waters around reefs in the warm tropical areas of the Indian and Pacific oceans.

The yellow-lipped sea krait Laticauda colubrina, widespread in coastal waters from the Bay of Bengal and the South China Sea to the islands of the western Pacific, basks on rocks or mangrove roots.

SEA SNAKES

These snakes are more aquatic than the sea kraits as they do not need to return to land to breed. In fact they have become so specialized for movement in the water that most are almost helpless on land. Most species are restricted to shallow coastal water, but the yellow-bellied sea snake is found far out to sea, drifting across the open oceans apparently at the mercy of the winds and currents.

CLASSIFICATION

ORDER SQUAMATA • SUBORDER SERPENTES • C. 18 FAMILIES C. 2,700 SPECIES • C. 450 GENERA FAMILY ELAPIDAE

Characteristics The body and tail are flattened from side to side to help them swim and their belly scales are usually very narrow. Their nostrils are on top of the snout, so they can breathe when most of the head is under the water, and they can be sealed by valves when the snake dives. The lung is much longer than in terrestrial snakes, and some species can take in oxygen from the water through skin. Glands at the base of the tongue excrete excess salt from the snake's bloodstream. Sea snakes are highly venomous.

Diet Most sea snakes feed on the fish around coral reefs and their eggs. The yellow-bellied sea snake relies on the tendency of small fish to gather under any floating object. When fish swarm under its tail, it swims backward, so they gather under its head, then it grabs them.

Reproduction The embryos remain in the female's body and she gives birth to live young.

Habitat Except for the yellow-bellied sea snake, these snakes are found from the Persian Gulf to the Western Pacific.

The yellow-bellied sea snake Pelamis platurus is the most widespread sea snake, from East Africa through the Pacific and Indian oceans to Central America.

TRUE VIPERS

Coiled beside a mammal trail, or in the branches of a fruiting tree where birds gather, or beside a desert shrub where lizards will come seeking shade, a viper is almost invisible because of its superb camouflage. Here it will wait for its prey to come within range. Some vipers actually lure prey within striking range by wriggling the insect-shaped tip of their tail.

Characteristics Most vipers are heavy-bodied, muscular snakes, with large heads. They have a single pair of very long, hollow fangs which are attached to a small bone on the upper jaw. This bone can rotate so that the fangs lie back along the length of the upper jaw when the snake's mouth is closed but can swing forward into striking position when the mouth is opened. Large jaw muscles squeeze the viper's very toxic venom from glands on either side of its head into the fangs which penetrate deep into the victim's body.

Diet Vipers feed on frogs, lizards, birds and small mammals. To kill their prey, vipers inject venom with one quick strike and then wait. Even if the animal runs away to die, the viper can follow its scent trail.

The rhinoceros viper Bitis nasicornis from Africa is one of the most colorful vipers, but its disruptive pattern makes it almost invisible in leaf litter.

Reproduction Some vipers lay eggs while others, especially those in very cold areas, give birth to live young. The pregnant females of these species—for example the European adder *Vipera berus* whose range extends into the bitter Arctic Circle—spend most of their time basking so the embryos can develop quickly in the short warm period. These females do not feed during this time and may become so emaciated that many die after they have given birth.

Habitat True vipers are found in an extremely wide range of habitats, from swamps and lake shores to deserts, from tropical rainforests to cold Arctic tundra. They are widely distributed in Asia, Africa, the Middle East and Europe.

CLASSIFICATION

ORDER SQUAMATA • SUBORDER SERPENTES • c. 18 FAMILIES c. 2,700 SPECIES • c. 450 GENERA FAMILY VIPERIDAE

TREE-DWELLING VIPER
The Usambara mountain viper *Atheris ceratophorus* of central Africa is one of eight species in its genus. They are commonly called leaf or bush vipers. Six of these are arboreal, with strong prehensile tails, large prominent heads and slender bodies. They are generally quite small, growing to about 2 feet (60 cm).

PIT VIPERS

The pit vipers are so named because of the deep pit between the eye and the nostril on each side of the head. Here there are sensory organs that detect heat. These organs are incredibly sensitive and can detect minute differences in temperature. They allow the pit vipers to locate warm-blooded prey, even on pitch-black nights.

Characteristics Like the true vipers, pit vipers are heavy-bodied, muscular snakes, with large heads and long, hollow fangs. The best known are the 30 species of rattlesnakes (genera *Crotalus* and *Sistrurus*) of North America, famous for the warning device on the tip of their tail. This rattle is formed from enlarged and thickened scale covers that are retained after molting and that hit against each other, producing the characteristic buzzing sound. Another North American pit viper, the cottonmouth or water moccasin *Agkistrodon piscivorus*, derives its common name from the white interior of its mouth which

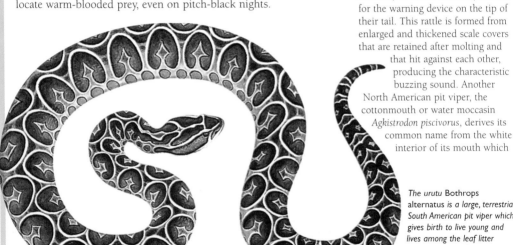

The urutu Bothrops alternatus *is a large, terrestrial South American pit viper which gives birth to live young and lives among the leaf litter on the rainforest floor.*

it gapes widely when threatened. The largest viper is the bushmaster *Lachesis muta* of Central and South America which grows to almost 13 feet (4 m) in length. The arboreal temple vipers (genus *Trimeresurus*) of Asia are mainly green in color and have prehensile tails.

Diet Pit vipers generally tend to hunt warm-blooded animals like rabbits, muskrats, ground squirrels, rats, mice and birds, but some take a wide range of food. The swamp-dwelling cottonmouth, for example, includes fish, frogs and other snakes in its diet. The bushmaster eats mainly mammals and is a classic ambush predator. It selects a suitable ambush site beside a mammal trail and waits, sometimes for weeks, until prey wanders within range.

Reproduction Some pit vipers lay eggs, others give birth to live young. One species, the mountain viper *Trimeresurus monticola* of South-East

Asia, remains coiled around or near the eggs until they hatch.

Habitat Most pit vipers live in forested regions and plantations, though some inhabit dry areas. Most species are terrestrial, some are tree-dwellers, and a few, like the cottonmouth which lives in swamps and beside lakes and streams, are semi-aquatic. Pit vipers are widely distributed throughout the Americas, Europe, Africa and Asia.

TEMPLE VIPERS
The green tree viper *Trimeresurus gramineus* is an Asian species.. Some vipers of this genus are known as "temple vipers." Because they are tractable and reluctant to bite humans, they are often kept in "snake temples" where they are freely handled and fed by the priests. Others are kept as good-luck charms in trees near villages. However, other species in the genus can be lethal to humans.

CLASSIFICATION

ORDER SQUAMATA • SUBORDER SERPENTES • C. 18 FAMILIES
C. 2,700 SPECIES • C. 450 GENERA
FAMILY VIPERIDAE

CLASSIFICATION TABLE

The classification of reptiles and frogs changes as new knowledge is acquired, and the most recent system is given below. However, in the species guide a simpler and more conventional system is used which includes all lizards in a single Suborder (Sauria) within the Order Squamata.

CLASS AMPHIBIA

SUBCLASS LISSAMPHIBIA

ORDER CAUDATA   **SALAMANDERS & NEWTS**

Suborder Sirenoidea

Sirenidae	Sirens

Suborder Cryptobranchoidea

Cryptobranchidae	Hellbenders & Giant Salamanders
Hynobiidae	Hynobiids

Suborder Salamandroidea

Amphiumidae	Amphiumas (Congo Eels)
Plethodontidae	Lungless Salamanders
Rhyacotritonidae	Torrent Salamanders
Proteidae	Mudpuppies, Waterdogs, & The Olm
Salamandridae	Salamandrids
Ambystomatidae	Mole Salamanders
Dicamptodontidae	Dicamptodontids

ORDER GYMNOPHIONA   **CAECILIANS**

Rhinatrematidae	South American Tailed Caecilians
Ichthyophiidae	Ichthyophiids
Uraeotyphlidae	Uraeotyphlids
Scolecomorphidae	Scolecomorphids
Caeciliidae	Caeciliids & Aquatic Caecilians

ORDER ANURA   **FROGS & TOADS**

Ascaphidae	"Tailed" Frogs
Leiopelmatidae	New Zealand Frogs
Bombinatoridae	Fire-Bellied Toads & Allies
Discoglossidae	Discoglossid Frogs
Pipidae	Pipas & "Clawed" Frogs
Rhinophrynidae	Cone-Nosed Frog
Megophryidae	Megophryids
Pelodytidae	Parsley Frogs
Pelobatidae	Spadefoots

/

Superfamily Bufonoidea

Allophrynidae	Allophrynid Frog
Brachycephalidae	Saddleback Frogs
Bufonidae	Toads
Helophrynidae	Ghost Frogs
Leptodactylidae	Neotropical Frogs
Myobatrachidae	Australasian Frogs
Sooglossiidae	Seychelles Frogs
Rhinodermatidae	Darwin's Frogs
Hylidae	Hylid Treefrogs
Pelodryadidae	Australasian Treefrogs
Centrolenidae	Glass Frogs
Pseudidae	Natator Frogs
Dendrobatidae	Dart-Poison Frogs

Superfamily Ranoidea

Microhylidae	Microhylids
Hemisotidae	Shovel-Nosed Frogs
Arthroleptidae	Squeakers
Ranidae	Ranid Frogs
Hyperoliidae	Reed & Lily Frogs
Rhacophoridae	Rhacaphorid Treefrogs

CLASS REPTILIA

SUBCLASS EUREPTILIA

SUPERORDER LEPIDOSAURIA

ORDER RHYNCHOCEPHALIA	TUATARAS
Sphenodontidae	Tuataras

ORDER SQUAMATA	SQUAMATES
Suborder Iguania	**Iguanid Lizards**
Corytophanidae	Helmeted Lizards
Crotaphytidae	Collared & Leopard Lizards
Hoplocercidae	Hoplocercids
Iguanidae	Iguanas
Opluridae	Madagascar Iguanians
Phrynosomatidae	Scaly, Sand & Horned Lizards
Polychrotidae	Anoloid Lizards
Tropiduridae	Tropidurids
Agamidae	Agamid Lizards
Chameleonidae	Chameleons

CLASSIFICATION TABLE continued

Suborder Scleroglossa

Superfamily Gekkonoidea

Eublepharidae	Eye-Lash Geckos
Gekkonidae	Geckos
Pygopodidae	Australasian Flapfoots

Superfamily Scincoidea

Xantusiidae	Night Lizards
Lacertidae	Lacertids
Scincidae	Skinks
Dibamidae	Dibamids
Cordylidae	Girdle-Tailed Lizards
Gerrhosauridae	Plated Lizards
Teiidae	Macroteiids
Gymnophthalmidae	Microteiids

Superfamily Anguoidea

Xenosauridae	Knob-Scaled Lizards
Anguidae	Anguids; Glass & Alligator Lizards

Helodermatidae	Beaded Lizards
Varanidae	Monitor Lizards
Lanthanotidae	Earless Monitor Lizard

Suborder Amphisbaenia — **Amphisbaenians**

Bipedidae	Ajolotes
Amphisbaenidae	Worm Lizards
Trogonophidae	Desert Ringed Lizards
Rhineuridae	Florida Worm Lizard

Suborder Serpentes — **Snakes**

Infraorder Scolecophidia

Anomalepididae	Blind Wormsnakes
Typhlopidae	Blind Snakes
Leptotyphlopidae	Thread Snakes

Infraorder Alethinophidia

Anomochelidae	Stump Heads
Aniliidae	Coral Pipesnakes

Cylindrophidae	Asian Pipesnakes
Uropeltidae	Shield Tails
Xenopeltidae	Sunbeam Snake
Loxocemidae	Dwarf Boa
Boidae	Pythons & Boas
Ungaliophiidae	Ungaliophiids
Bolyeriidae	Round Island Snakes
Tropidophiidae	Woodsnakes
Acrochordidae	File Snakes
Atractaspididae	Mole Vipers
Colubridae	Harmless & Rear-Fanged Snakes
Elapidae	Cobras, Kraits, Coral Snakes & Sea Snakes
Viperidae	Adders & Vipers

SUPERORDER TESTUDINES

ORDER TESTUDINATA	**TURTLES, TERRAPINS & TORTOISES**

Suborder Pleurodira	**Side-Neck Turtles**
Chelidae	Snake-Neck Turtles
Pelomedusidae	Helmeted Side-Neck Turtles

Suborder Cryptodira	**Hidden-Necked Turtles**

Superfamily Trionychoidea

Kinosternidae	Mud & Musk Turtles
Dermatemydidae	Mesoamerican River Turtle
Carretochelyidae	Australian Softshell Turtle
Trionychidae	Holarctic & Paleotropical Softshell Turtles

Superfamily Cheloniodea

Dermochelyidae	Leatherback Sea Turtles
Cheloniidae	Sea Turtles

Superfamily Testudinoidea

Chelydridae	Snapping Turtles
Emydidae	New World Pond Turtles & Terrapins
Testudinidae	Tortoises
Bataguridae	Old World Pond Turtles

SUPERORDER ARCHOSAURIA

ORDER CROCODILIA	**CROCODILIANS**
Alligatoridae	Alligators & Caimans
Crocodylidae	Crocodiles
Gavialidae	Gharials

INDEX

Page references in *italics* indicate illustrations and photos.

ACKNOWLEDGMENTS

TEXT The text for this publication has been drawn from research provided by Aaron M. Bauer, Charles C. Carpenter, Harold G. Cogger, Caroline Colton (index), William E. Duellman, Carl Gans, Brian Groombridge, Harold Heatwole, Benedetto Lanza, William E. Magnusson, Donald G. Newman, Annamaria Nistri, Ronald A. Nussbaum, Fritz Jurgen Obst, Olivier C. Rieppel, Charles A. Ross, Jay M. Savage, Richard Shine, Stefano Vanni

ILLUSTRATIONS Alistar Barnard, Anne Bowman, Simone End, Christer Eriksson, John Francis, Mike Gorman, John Gittoes, Tim Hayward, Robert Hynes, David Kirshner, Frank Knight, James McKinnon, Colin Newman, Tony Pyrzakowski, Barbara Rodanska, Trevor Ruth, Peter Schouten

PHOTOGRAPHS Australian Museum, Bruce Coleman Limited, Corel Corporation, NHPA

CONSULTANT EDITOR Dr. Harold G. Cogger is the John Evans Memorial Fellow at the Australian Museum, Sydney, and Conjoint Professor, Faculty of Science and Mathematics, University of Newcastle, Australia